AMERICA'S DUMBEST ★DATES★

OVER 500 TALES OF FUMBLED FLIRTATIONS

Merry Bloch Jones

Andrews McMeel Publishing

Kansas City

America's Dumbest Dates

Copyright © 1998 by Merry Bloch Jones. All rights reserved.
Printed in the United States of America.
No part of this book may be used or reproduced in any manner
whatsoever without written permission except in the case of
reprints in the context of reviews. For information, write
Andrews McMeel Publishing, an Andrews McMeel Universal company,
4520 Main Street, Kansas City, Missouri 64111.

www.andrewsmcmeel.com
98 99 00 01 BRG 10 9 8 7 6 5 4 3 2 1
Book design by Jill Weber of Frajil Farms.
Book typeset by Steve Brooker of Just Your Type.

Library of Congress Cataloging-in-Publication Data
Jones, Merry Bloch.
    America's dumbest dates : over 500 tales of fumbled flirtations /
Merry Bloch Jones.
        p.   cm.
    ISBN 0-8362-6769-9 (pbk)
    1. Dating (Social customs)—Humor. 2. Courtship—Humor.
I. Title.
PN6231.D3J66   1998
818'.540208—dc21   98-26462
                                                          CIP

ATTENTION: SCHOOLS AND BUSINESSES

Andrews McMeel books are available at quantity discounts with bulk
purchase for educational, business, or sales promotional use. For
information, please write to: Special Sales Department, Andrews
McMeel Publishing, 4520 Main Street, Kansas City, Missouri 64111.

CONTENTS

To Robin, my best date

ACKNOWLEDGMENTS

Thanks to my agent, Stedman Mays; my editor, Nora Donaghy; the men and women across the country who contributed their stories with candor and enthusiasm; Shannon Guder, Lanie Zera, Susan Stone, Susan Collins, Susan Small, Ileana Stevens, Michael Cory, Michael and Jan Molinaro, Nancy Delman, Jane Braun, Janet Martin, Judy Bloch, and, especially, Robin, Baille, and Neely.

INTRODUCTION

We've all been there. Anyone who's ever been single and dated for any length of time has undoubtedly had at least one. Most of us have had dozens. Even hundreds. Sometimes they come in clusters, like a rash. Other times, like a persistent pimple, you can't get rid of a single, isolated one. Whether you're careful and cautious or brave and bodacious, you're still likely to get some. No matter where you hang out, what you do for a living, whether you're male or female, old or young—if you're single and out there, sooner or later, you're going to be stuck with at least one Dumb Date.

As singles fend their ways through jungles of blind dates and bad matches, they are likely to confront dumbness as they never imagined it. While dating, they learn that dumbness can take many forms, can spring anywhere, any time, without warning. It can appear shamelessly in the eyes of the public or secretly in those of the beholder. And it can be potent enough to render full-grown, articulate adults speechless, even to make them panic and run.

This is not to say that dating is by definition dumb. Plenty of singles have great dates; many

eventually marry or commit to people they've dated. Thousands live happily ever after, perhaps looking back nostalgically at their dumbest dates.

Nonetheless, every day, multitudes of singles endure dismally dumb dates, finding themselves paired with partners who crack their knuckles or their gum, bounce their knees, bite their nails, whine through their noses, whistle through their teeth, mutter, hum, sing, smoke, spit, curse, complain, flex, are tattooed or pierced all over, drive like maniacs or mules, eat like pigs or parakeets, act too aggressive or too passive, wear too much cologne or not enough deodorant, grow too much or not enough hair, dress like aliens or accountants.

★ ★ ★ ★ ★ ★ ★ ★ ★ ★ ★ ★ ★ ★

What exactly is a dumb date? How do we define and quantify it? For the purposes of this book, we start by saying that dumb dates are never nasty or hurtful; they're more often merely clueless or clumsy. Dumbness on dates is often unintentional, accidental, invisible to the perpetrator. And it can usually be identified as something that, if a third party were present, observing your date, you would turn to that person and say, "Do you *believe* this?"

This book explores the nature of dumb dates. In these pages, endurers of dumb behaviors and situations speak out and describe them candidly, graphically, and mercilessly. It is our hope that singles reading it will be assured that they are not alone in confronting the dumb date

★★★★★★★★★★★★

phenomenon—perhaps, by comparison, their own encounters will seem less drastic. We hope, too, that readers in committed relationships will find renewed appreciation of their partners; without them, they'd probably be out there, dealing with dumb dates.

About four hundred people across the country contributed their stories to this book. They range in age from eighteen to almost eighty, old enough to have had at least a few years of dating experience. They are middle- and upper-middle-class people of many religions and racial and ethnic backgrounds. Among them are teachers, psychologists, doctors, dentists, lawyers, construction workers, chemists, painters, accountants, bankers, nurses, office managers, administrators, architects,

★ ★ ★ ★ ★ ★ ★ ★ ★ ★ ★ ★ ★ ★

planners, interior designers, a dietitian, a maintenance worker, hairdressers, truck drivers, shopkeepers, social workers, consultants, a real estate agent, a travel agent, talent agents, editors, students, journalists, mechanics, delivery people, salespeople, homemakers, photographers, administrators, computer specialists, a mailman, a judge, a horticulturist, a historian, and a librarian.

Because men and women are forever destined to try to get it together, the process of their trying is eternally interesting. Married or single, male or female, most of us want to know what others go through in finding a mate. This book gives us intimate glimpses into that process, lets us peek into other people's private

★★★★★★★★★★★★★

dating moments, and provides insight about how otherwise bright and successful people can completely blow their chances for romantic relationships by doing something really dumb.

Those who contributed their stories doubt that their dumbest dates will recognize themselves in and learn from what they read here. But they hope that their stories will satisfy others that, no matter how dumb it gets out there, it can always get seriously dumber.

★ ★ ★ ★ ★ ★ ★ ★ ★ ★ ★ ★ ★ ★ 7

★First★
Impressions

Ever since childhood, we've been warned about them. They're why we scrub our faces, shake hands firmly, and smile broadly. They're why we dress for success, why we pull in our stomachs and push out our chests. They are first impressions, and they mean everything. For the sake of first impressions, we scrape the dirt from under our fingernails, shine our shoes, polish our teeth, suck breath mints, and spray ourselves with all sorts of scents.

No matter how we try to control matters, though, there are times when we blow it. We sometimes seem more klutzy than confident, more smarmy than smooth. While strutting our stuff, sooner or later, we inevitably slip on one of life's banana peels and, however sophisticated or charismatic we are, despite our savvy savoir faire, end up on our behinds.

"I wanted to impress Jeff," Meg recalls, "so I insisted on driving. I got into the driver's seat and, with infinite grace and aplomb, slammed my hand in the car door. My fingers swelled up like golf balls. We spent our date in the emer-

★ ★ ★ ★ ★ ★ ★ ★ ★ ★ ★ ★ ★

gency room, where I got my rings cut off and fourteen stitches in my pinkie. He was impressed, believe me."

For better or worse, our first impressions are often unforgettable—especially in the world of dating, where our efforts are handicapped by nervousness, doubts, stresses, and hopes (and, all too often, dumbness).

When Walt asked me out, he said I should cook and he'd bring the entertainment. Turned out he was an Amway salesman. The "entertainment" was their packaged presentation. It wasn't enough that I'd cooked; he wanted me to buy his detergent, too.

AMY, 30, BALTIMORE, MD.

★★★★★★★★★★★★★

For our first date, I invited Joe to dinner. He brought Tupperware, to take home the leftovers.

SOPHIE, 55, CHERRY HILL, N.J.

Howard didn't want to date me; he wanted to date my skirt. When he asked me out, I was wearing this skintight, lime-green suede miniskirt. When he came to get me, his face fell. He pouted and asked, "Where's the skirt?"

GIGI, 35, VILLANOVA, PA.

★ ★ ★ ★ ★ ★ ★ ★ ★ ★ ★ ★ ★

When she opened the door, I was expecting her to be someone else. I'd met her and her girl-friend at the same time and I'd intended to call the other one. I got their names mixed up. I tried to explain, and she threw me out.

ETHAN, 23, BOCA RATON, FLA.

In her personal ad, she'd described herself as having a "great mind, greater body. Stunning." By "great," she must have meant "large." But she was right about the stunning part. I was quite stunned. In fact, I was speechless.

LOUIS, 37, NEW ORLEANS, LA.

★ ★ ★ ★ ★ ★ ★ ★ ★ ★ ★ ★ ★

Lance invited me over for a drink. The door was open. He yelled, "Come in," and greeted me, wearing nothing but a silk smoking jacket. It struck me as funny, and I burst out laughing. He made me a drink and sat there, in the jacket and his birthday suit, acting as if everything was completely normal. We talked. I had a couple of drinks and left. Neither of us mentioned the fact that he was naked. Actually, he was a perfect gentleman.

SALLY, 33, RICHMOND, VA.

★ ★ ★ ★ ★ ★ ★ ★ ★ ★ ★ ★ ★ **15**

When he asked me out, he was wearing a baseball cap. When he came to get me, he wasn't wearing it. I didn't recognize him. He was completely bald, not a hair on his head. Not an eyebrow.

ERIN, 24, CASPER, WYO.

★ ★ ★ ★ ★ ★ ★ ★ ★ ★ ★ ★ ★ ★

Ben took me out and introduced me to his car. "This is Suzy," he said. "Isn't she beautiful? She's not just a Trans Am. She's my baby." Then he stroked the hood.

BETH, 27, ITHACA, N.Y.

In anticipation of our date, Curtis sent me poetry—about eternal love, reincarnation, knowing me in another lifetime. Fate and destiny. It was scary. Especially the meter.

RUTH, 30, DENVER, COLO.

★★★★★★★★★★★★★★ 17

I hired a guy to write a brochure for work. The guy messed up the job and missed the deadline, so I chewed him out and fired him—and guess who my blind date was the next Saturday night?

DODIE, 36, GALVESTON, TEX.

I got fixed up with the same guy twice. He was just as boring the second time. The first date was so dull that neither of us had even remembered the other's name.

MARCIA, 35, WASHINGTON, D.C.

★ ★ ★ ★ ★ ★ ★ ★ ★ ★ ★ ★

Our first date, Wes brought his buddy along. They sat shoulder to shoulder, snickered at private jokes, whispered. I wondered, What am I doing here? And then, when they both dropped me off, Wes asked if I wanted to go out again next week.

LYNDA, 23, PROVIDENCE, R.I.

★★★★★★★★★★★★★★

On our first date, as he walked toward me for the first time, I saw that he had no right arm. I was upset, wondering what could have happened to him. A car accident? Bone cancer? It was such a shame. I tried hard not to let my eyes drift down to where his arm should have been; I didn't want him to feel self-conscious. But I was nervous. I stuttered, babbled, heard myself sound absolutely brainless as we greeted each other. Finally, he said, "Well, we ought to get going," and from behind his back, his right arm suddenly appeared to guide me to the car. I was stunned. Speechless. He might as well have pulled out a herd of elephants. Or a dozen naked ladies. I was in a cold sweat, traumatized, and our date hadn't even started yet.

LESLIE, 28, SEATTLE, WASH.

20 ★ ★ ★ ★ ★ ★ ★ ★ ★ ★ ★ ★ ★ ★

So there I am, telling her about my pal Al, who we're going to double with. And guess who her first heartthrob was? Guess who broke her heart in tenth grade? Guess who never got over it?

WARREN, 32, WEST MONROE, LA.

After our first date, Gary left a Polaroid of his erection on my windshield—with a note telling me to call him when I was ready to go out again.

LINDA, 39, ATLANTA, GA.

★ ★ ★ ★ ★ ★ ★ ★ ★ ★ ★ ★ ★ ★

When I got home, I realized that the back seam of my pants had split wide open. Did it happen when I sat down in the car to come home, after I'd put on my jacket? Or had it happened earlier? The whole time we were at the party, did everyone have a view of my panties? My date said nothing to me about it; was he laughing behind my behind?

RENEE, 22, FORT LAUDERDALE, FLA.

The "friend" who fixed me up with Luigi neglected to tell me that he spoke no English—well, except, "Kiss me quick."

CARLA, 44, MICHIGAN CITY, MICH.

★ ★ ★ ★ ★ ★ ★ ★ ★ ★ ★ ★ ★

Paul asked me out by giving me a list of several professional or formal social functions to attend— not by inviting me to a movie, or to have a drink. When I said I'd like to spend our first date alone so we could get to know each other, he took out his calendar and said his first free weekend was in July, seven months away.

CAROLYN, 36, BOSTON, MASS.

★★★★★★★★★★★★★ 23

I got fixed up with my ex-husband. Hadn't seen him in fourteen years. He'd gained about forty pounds, lost his hair. And I guess he needs glasses, because he didn't even recognize me. I had to *tell* him who I was. Shortest date I ever had.

COLLEEN, 55, CASPER, WYO.

★★★★★★★★★★★★★

Julie brought her Chihuahua along. It looked like a half-starved rat and rode in a little bag she had specially made for it. She told me she takes him everywhere. If he can't go someplace, she won't either. Whenever I came close to her, the thing growled, and Julie cooed, "Oh, precious poochie's so protective of Mommy." And she fed him morsels of her dinner. I paid for the dog to eat veal Oscar.

REED, 31, ATLANTA, GA.

The earring in her eyebrow? Well, okay. The one in her tongue? Goodnight.

ED, 27, BALTIMORE, MD.

★ ★ ★ ★ ★ ★ ★ ★ ★ ★ ★ ★ ★ ★ ★ **25**

Amber's mother came with us on our date. It started out that she asked if I could drop her mom at her apartment, but on the way, Mama mentioned that she was dying for a steak, and before I knew it, I was watching her chow down on a blood-red New York strip. She and Amber chattered and yammered. They had a grand time. I didn't get a word in edgewise, until the waitress asked who'd take the check.

WEBSTER, 29, KNOXVILLE, TENN.

★ ★ ★ ★ ★ ★ ★ ★ ★ ★ ★ ★ ★

He showed up in a pink suit and told me not to call him "Jeff"; he preferred "Flash." When he wanted my attention, he grunted or made animal sounds. And he complained about my clothes, that I should loosen up and wear something with feathers.

STELLA, 47, TALLAHASSEE, FLA.

When he asked me out he was wearing a three-piece suit. When he picked me up, he was in leather pants, torn shirt, denim vest, a Nazi helmet, and he was riding a Harley.

MARIE, 24, LITTLE ROCK, ARK.

★ ★ ★ ★ ★ ★ ★ ★ ★ ★ ★ ★ ★ ★ 27

I was late for our first date—really late, like maybe four hours. And it was her birthday. So she got mad and, I guess, rightfully so. But I ring the doorbell and the first thing I know, the door opens and there's a pie in my face. I saw it coming, but had no time to duck. Whipped cream was coming out of my nose. What could I do? I grabbed her, kissed her, and licked whipped cream.

LES, 29, FORT MYERS, FLA.

★ ★ ★ ★ ★ ★ ★ ★ ★ ★ ★ ★ ★ ★

Her mom entertained me in the living room, explained that Justine was running late, finishing with an earlier "appointment" in the family room. Her mom explained that Justine was systematic, determined to get what she wanted, and had lined up two or three dates a night until she'd found the right man.

FLOYD, 24, CINCINNATI, OHIO

★★★★★★★★★★★★★★ 29

She gave me lousy directions, so I got lost on the way to her house. I called from the car and got even lousier directions. I called again, and finally she had her roommate give me directions. By the time I got there, I'd been in the car almost two hours. I was sweaty and wasted, and she had an attitude because I was late. She greeted me, "Finally. I was about to give up and go out with my friends."

NED, 34, BETHESDA, MD.

★ ★ ★ ★ ★ ★ ★ ★ ★ ★ ★ ★ ★ ★ ★

Ira asked me why I didn't wear false eyelashes, and he suggested that I wear heavier foundation. A lot more makeup.

CATHRYN, 27, DES MOINES, IOWA

He cracked his knuckles once every seven seconds through the whole movie. As soon as you thought he was done, that maybe he was going to relax, he'd crack them again.

BARBARA, 27, RALEIGH, N.C.

He sat on my couch bouncing his knee so hard I thought he'd take off. The floor was shaking. The vase was rattling on the coffee table; balls were dropping off the pussy willows. At the movie, he had the whole row of seats bouncing. When I got home, I couldn't stop vibrating.

RITA, 29, PITTSBURGH, PA.

★★★★★★★★★★★★★

He couldn't keep his hands out of his pants pockets. I kept thinking, What's he doing? Then I thought, I really don't want to know.

MICHELLE, 28, WILMINGTON, DEL.

We went to her apartment. Everything was blue. Walls, carpet, counters. Towels, plates, bedding, curtains, furniture. The artwork had blue tones. She had a sculpture, some kind of blue glass. I went to the bathroom. Her toothbrush was blue. It was then that I noticed what she was wearing—blue clothes. Blue nail polish. There was something wrong.

DEAN, 20, CHARLOTTE, N.C.

★ ★ ★ ★ ★ ★ ★ ★ ★ ★ ★ ★ ★ ★

Kara had long straight hair, braided on one side. Her apartment was lit with candles, and incense was burning. There were crystals and pyramids and lava lamps. She offered me marijuana. All she needed was sitar music and I'd have thought I'd time-warped into the sixties.

BEN, 49, SYRACUSE, N.Y.

Frank carried a mirror and hairbrush, hairspray, cologne, and even a blow-dryer in his glove compartment. And before he got out of the car, he used them all.

BECKIE, 37, ROSEMONT, PA.

★★★★★★★★★★★★★★

He came into my apartment and said, "What a classy place. How much's it run ya?" He also asked, during the evening, how much I pay in taxes, how old I am, and how much I pay for a monthly parking spot. Oh yes—and if the stones in my ring were real.

PAM, 54, SAN FRANCISCO, CALIF.

★ ★ ★ ★ ★ ★ ★ ★ ★ ★ ★ ★ ★ 35

She kept dead flowers. She had a bouquet from her friend's wedding that she said was six or seven years ago. A dozen roses from some ancient Valentine's Day. A few dead corsages from her high school proms. I asked about them; she gave me a tour.

SAM, 26, OMAHA, NEBR.

★★★★★★★★★★★★★

Rick showed me around his house, pointed out how he kept his clothes in perfect order, everything facing the same way, arranged by color and fabric. His decor was perfect. The fringe on his rugs was even. His books were arranged alphabetically, by subject and author; his CDs by group. His oven was shiny and grease-free. He was very proud of all this. It scared me to death.

ABBEY, 33, DALLAS, TEX.

★ ★ ★ ★ ★ ★ ★ ★ ★ ★ ★ ★ ★ 37

Hope had long black hair, was dressed in long black clothes. Her nail polish was black. Even her lipstick was black. I asked her if black was her favorite color and she said, "It's just who I am. I'm a creature of darkness." So I asked her if she sucked blood. She just looked at me, didn't smile. And her eyes were very, very dark.

CHUCK, 29, AUSTIN, TEX.

The music was soft. The evening was cool. She was beautiful. I pulled her closer to me and held her. She asked me to stop breathing on her eyeballs.

JAMES, 29, LANSING, MICH.

★ ★ ★ ★ ★ ★ ★ ★ ★ ★ ★ ★ ★

Bonnie collected dolls. All sizes, all shapes. She sewed clothes for them. Her shelves and furniture were covered with them. As we left to go out, she patted one on the head and told it she wouldn't be late. Scary.

CLIFF, 34, TUCSON, ARIZ.

Tom tried to win my kids over. He arrived with candy and baseball cards. And he called my son "dude," punched his shoulder, and asked, "S'happnin'?"

STACEY, 32, RALEIGH, N.C.

★ ★ ★ ★ ★ ★ ★ ★ ★ ★ ★ ★ ★ ★ ★ 39

His pitch was that he was married. To him, that was a strong point. We could date, flirt, have dinner, romance, sex. And then, best of all, he'd *leave* so I wouldn't have to do his laundry, sew his buttons, or clean his whiskers out of my sink. I could put on loud music and dance around my apartment, rearrange the furniture, read, do whatever I wanted, unencumbered.

GRACE, 30, CLEVELAND, OHIO

★ ★ ★ ★ ★ ★ ★ ★ ★ ★ ★ ★ ★ ★

He wore a lot of cologne. When I got close to him it was like getting assaulted by some high-voltage scent. My nostrils burned. I smelled it in my clothes afterward. I took a shower, just to wash it out of my pores. My apartment smelled like him for a week.

EVELYN, 37, NORTH PROVIDENCE, R.I.

★★★★★★★★★★★★★★★ 41

Susan left her sweater at my place. She came back the next day to get it and left her scarf. She came back the next day to get it and left her library book. By the time she came back for the gloves she left when she got the book, we were having a relationship.

JULIUS, 33, MADISON, WIS.

★ ★ ★ ★ ★ ★ ★ ★ ★ ★ ★ ★

She hadn't worn her glasses, so I had no idea she needed them. When she put Parmesan cheese instead of sugar in her tea, I thought, well, both shakers look alike—it could happen to anyone. But when she came back from the ladies' room and sat with the guy in the next booth, I figured something was wrong. Turns out she had no idea what I looked like. He was dressed in the same colored shirt, so she figured he was me. She couldn't see a thing.

RICK, 40, DOVER, DEL.

★★★★★★★★★★★★★★★ 43

She seemed attractive enough to me, but my dog hated her. As soon as I brought her through the door, he growled, bared his teeth, and snarled. Foamed at the mouth. I've never seen anything like it.

ELLIOT, 28, WAUKEGAN, ILL.

She started out by warning me that she had PMS so I'd better not get on her nerves. The whole night, anything I did or said, she went, "Tsk." Or sometimes she said, "Oh, please."

JEREMY, 28, DENVER, COLO.

★ ★ ★ ★ ★ ★ ★ ★ ★ ★ ★ ★ ★

First date: We go drinking. He walks me home, asks to use the bathroom. He doesn't come out, so I go look and find him passed out on my bed, drunk. I can't wake him up and he's too heavy to move. So there I am, wide awake, with this huge, luscious, gorgeous guy in my bed, unconscious. It was awful. Like having your jaw wired at a pie-eating contest.

MYRA, 37, MILWAUKEE, WIS.

★ ★ ★ ★ ★ ★ ★ ★ ★ ★ ★ ★ ★ ★

He kept peeking over his shoulder, my shoulder, past me, around the restaurant. I thought, Is he afraid to look at me? Are the cops chasing him? Is he wanted for something? Is he a thief? A hit man? Or is he looking out for his girlfriend? Is he married? Afraid to be seen with me? What? He never met my eyes once the whole time. If he were to see me again, there's no way he'd recognize me.

LAURIE, 31, SEATTLE, WASH.

★ ★ ★ ★ ★ ★ ★ ★ ★ ★ ★ ★ ★

It was icy. I slipped on the side-walk. Instinctively, I grabbed on to Myrna for support, and she fell on top of me. I got up and tried to help her up, but she pulled me back down. We ended up crawling to the car on our hands and knees like Laurel and Hardy.

CARL, 25, SOUTHFIELD, MICH.

★ ★ ★ ★ ★ ★ ★ ★ ★ ★ ★ ★ ★ ★ ★ 47

In line at the movie, he looked pale. He explained that he was always nervous on first dates and had had a nosebleed on the way over. Then he fainted. Flat on the sidewalk. The theater called the paramedics. Someone gave him smelling salts. When he came to, he asked for a rain check and said next time wouldn't be our first date anymore, so he wouldn't be as nervous.

GINGER, 27, ATLANTA, GA.

★ ★ ★ ★ ★ ★ ★ ★ ★ ★ ★ ★ ★

Driving to the shore, I bought Dena some coffee. Apparently, she decided not to finish it and tossed half of it out the window—except that the window was closed at the time. So she was covered with hot coffee. And so was my window, the seat, and the carpet of my car.

MIKE, 37, MEDFORD, N.J.

She looked a bit queasy. When I asked if she felt all right, she said she was a little bit nervous; first date and all. Then she threw up on the front seat of my car. I'll never get rid of the smell.

GREG, 27, CLEVELAND, OHIO

★ ★ ★ ★ ★ ★ ★ ★ ★ ★ ★ ★ ★ ★ 49

At the end of the night, I was tired. I drove to her house, got out, and came around to get her. She looked baffled, asked where we were going. And, oops—I realized I'd taken her to my old girlfriend's house. Force of habit. I tried to laugh it off, but she wasn't fooled. I was only glad she'd said something before I walked her to the door.

PETE, 26, DENVER, COLO.

★★★★★★★★★★★★★★

We went to a party and he got slobbering drunk, slurred his words, and took off his shoes to show me his Odor-eaters. Someone had to take him home; I got a ride with one of his friends. The next day, he called to ask me out again.

PIPER, 24, OCONOMOWOC, WIS.

Oh, dear. He did tricks with his scalp, wiggled his ears, and touched his nose with his tongue.

SHIRLEY, 41, BETHESDA, MD.

★ ★ ★ ★ ★ ★ ★ ★ ★ ★ ★ ★ ★ ★ 51

CHAPTER TWO

★ The Art of ★
Conversation

While dating, people communicate in lots of ways, few of which involve actual talking. Nevertheless, when we go out with someone, talking is the customary way we break the ice. We try to get to know each other through chitchat, small talk, and banter; as our interest grows, we progress to flattery, innuendoes of intimacy, double entendres and, sometimes, sweet nothings.

Those skilled at dating develop a cadre of conversational techniques ranging from the directly disarming to the coyly charming, from open flirting to evasive skirting. And, because date conversation involves much more than compiled words and sentences, successful daters must become masters of body language, intonation, intuition, implication, interpretation, and timing.

Through conversation, we and our dates try to match our rhythms and find out if we're in sync, and if we have common or at least compatible styles. Not that this proves anything: Words are

★ ★ ★ ★ ★ ★ ★ ★ ★ ★ ★ ★ ★

only words. But, by employing their beauty or bluntness, their clauses and pauses, we can talk our way to romance. Or send it running.

Right up front, as I'm twirling my pasta, he announces that he's bisexual. Actually, he says, he likes men more than women. But he'd like to have a family. All he'd really need are Friday nights and occasional summer Sundays off, with no questions asked. What did I say? Was I interested?

PAMELA, 23, TAOS, N.MEX.

★★★★★★★★★★★★★★

He started the evening by telling me about his prison record. About life on the inside. He thought this was entertaining.

LISA, 33, DETROIT, MICH.

On our first date, as soon as we get in the car, Daryl announces that the cold sore on his mouth is only a cold sore, nothing more. "Believe me," he says, "it has nothing to do with what's below my waist."

ANDREA, 27, WASHINGTON, D.C.

★ ★ ★ ★ ★ ★ ★ ★ ★ ★ ★ ★ ★ **57**

I asked Camille to tell me about herself. She told me she'd died during the Black Plague, been killed on the guillotine during the French Revolution, helped with the Underground Railroad before the Civil War, and had been a personal slave to some Egyptian pharaoh, but she couldn't remember which one—it was so long ago. She told me the names she went by in several of her incarnations and detailed a star-crossed love affair with a man of the wrong caste in India. She asked if I was in touch with my past lives. When I told her I was having enough trouble with this one, she told me I was spiritually a child.

MARTIN, 28, LITTLE ROCK, ARK.

★ ★ ★ ★ ★ ★ ★ ★ ★ ★ ★ ★

I noticed Marian in church and, after the service, I was amazed when she walked up to me and said that the Lord had told her that I was going to be her husband. So I took her to dinner. I had to go out with her; I'm sure I'll have to marry her. Who's going to argue with the Lord?

PETER, 26, RICHMOND, VA.

★★★★★★★★★★★★★★ 59

Before we'd ordered drinks, he announced that he was never getting married again, so if marriage was what I wanted, we'd better quit right then. I asked if I could find out his last name before I decided. He sparred with me. Interpreted everything as manipulation. Asked me how much time I spent putting on my makeup. Accused women of "setting traps" for men. When I objected to the generalization, he asked if I was one of those ball-busting feminists.

WENDY, 42, TAMPA, FLA.

60 ★ ★ ★ ★ ★ ★ ★ ★ ★ ★ ★ ★ ★ ★

First date: Waiting for dessert, he said, "I'm mostly impotent, but I'd like to get married. What do you say?"

CALLIE, 23, MINNEAPOLIS, MINN.

He started the conversation by saying that he wasn't the type for monogamy, and that I shouldn't expect marriage. If that's what I wanted, he wasn't for me. "Look, I don't want to get in your way— you gotta do what you gotta do." He was breaking up with me before we even went out.

LILY, 32, SEATTLE, WASH.

★ ★ ★ ★ ★ ★ ★ ★ ★ ★ ★ ★ ★ ★ ★ 61

When Paige found out I was an attorney, she went ballistic. She chewed me out, said her lawyer was an imbecile, and said her ex-husband's was a scoundrel who got away with ripping her off in their divorce settlement and it was somehow my fault because I was a lawyer, too.

BURTON, 41, LAKE FOREST, ILL.

★★★★★★★★★★★★★

He confessed that he was married, but that his wife was in a nursing home permanently, having suffered a severe stroke years ago. Nice try, I thought. I happen to know the lady; she's in my book club.

SYLVIA, 57, KANSAS CITY, MO.

Adrian started our date by announcing she was going to have a child. No, she wasn't pregnant. She was in the process of picking the father. Was I interested?

MICHAEL, 27, ESCONDIDO, CALIF.

★ ★ ★ ★ ★ ★ ★ ★ ★ ★ ★ ★ ★ ★

All he could talk about was money. The cost of new cars, running shoes, the overhead in his business. His financial plans, including his assessment of his tax situation, didn't make for a very romantic conversation (although I did learn about a new tax-exempt investment fund).

ERNESTINE, 24, DENVER, COLO.

★ ★ ★ ★ ★ ★ ★ ★ ★ ★ ★ ★ ★

All through our date, Gary talked about his business. Like I cared about his prospect list or how many air-conditioning units he intended to sell this year.

KIM, ST. LOUIS, MO.

Every other word was a curse word. Specifically, the "f" word. The man could not make a sentence, not express a coherent thought without putting "effing" in front of it.

BRITTANY, 25, TOLEDO, OHIO

★★★★★★★★★★★★★

Joel complained at length about how women hit on him. They'd ask for his number, call him at home, at work. Fax him. Beg him to tie them up, use handcuffs. Offer to pay him for his sexual services. Poor guy. He was so tired. I made sure he got home early and told him to take his phone off the hook.

PENNY, 33, CHEYENNE, WYO.

Rachel kept correcting my English. "Not 'who'; 'whom.'" Or "Not 'me'; 'I.'" She complained about my so-called "accent." It was like being out with your English teacher.

JOE, 38, BROOKLYN, N.Y.

★ ★ ★ ★ ★ ★ ★ ★ ★ ★ ★ ★ ★

All Stan talked about was food. The nuance of bay leaf in the brisket. The color of the wine. The texture of the watercress. He talked about every item on the menu. He read it and reread it. Aloud, like poetry.

BENITA, 46, GARY, IND.

★ ★ ★ ★ ★ ★ ★ ★ ★ ★ ★ ★ ★ ★ 67

Being out with Trevor was like taking a psychological test. He asked why I chose each word I spoke—why did I say "pasta" instead of "spaghetti," stuff like that. He asked why I wore mascara, why I prefer flats to heels—was I upset about being tall? I felt probed, like someone was invading my skull.

LORENE, 41, FRAMINGHAM, MASS.

Every date with Roger was like the first—because he never listened. Never remembered anything I'd said.

IRENE, 34, SAGINAW, MICH.

★ ★ ★ ★ ★ ★ ★ ★ ★ ★ ★ ★ ★

Jill spoke MBA. She wanted to "prioritize our activities" so we could "maximize our time." A relationship would "impact" on her life plan. Her parents "make a great team." Maddening.

CALVIN, 38, SWARTHMORE, PA.

Our date was like a job interview. He wanted to know what I wanted from life, where I wanted to be in five years, ten years. Which I valued more: security or opportunity. He asked me to write my epitaph. I said, "Here lies Marilyn. She dated her share of jerks." He laughed.

MARILYN, 34, HOUSTON, TEX.

★ ★ ★ ★ ★ ★ ★ ★ ★ ★ ★ ★ ★ ★ 69

Phoebe tried to sound intelligent. She used a lot of syllables, but the wrong words. I called a kid who works for me impudent, and she shook her head. "Now wait just a minute," she said. "Just because you don't like him doesn't mean he can't get it *up*."

BRIAN, 29, DALLAS, TEX.

70 ★ ★ ★ ★ ★ ★ ★ ★ ★ ★ ★ ★

She was a Scientologist and tried to sell me on it. I'm talking relentless, high-pressure techniques. She was like a pit bull, not letting go. There are used car salesmen who could learn a lot from her.

DREW, 34, SACRAMENTO, CALIF.

Elise looked into my eyes and warned me not to get involved with her. "When I have strong feelings for someone," she said, "I interfere with their aura. It's unintentional. I can't help it, but I'm sort of an emotional stalker. I sap their energy."

RICK, 33, BETHESDA, MD.

★★★★★★★★★★★★★ 71

Florence said whatever came into her mind. It was amazing. I'd never imagined that a human being could have so many thoughts, let alone form so many sentences, about so little.

DYLAN, 44, ST. PAUL, MINN.

Stan showed me that he had "Stacey" on his arm and pulled up his sleeve to show me "Brenda" on his shoulder. Then he winked and declared that he'd saved the spot over his heart for me.

VALERIE, 23, KNOXVILLE, TENN.

★ ★ ★ ★ ★ ★ ★ ★ ★ ★ ★ ★ ★ ★

Jay was quiet. No, that's not it. Jay didn't speak. He *could,* he just didn't. If you enjoy dead silence, he's the guy for you. When I wanted chitchat, I had to create it myself. He was an excellent listener. But when I ran out of monologue, there was Jay, with no response. After our date, he called me on the phone, said hello, and waited for me to talk.

SARA, 26, CHICAGO, ILL.

★★★★★★★★★★★★★★ 73

Over cocktails, he declared that he was still only separated, not divorced, that he had herpes and had had a vasectomy. Then he said, "Now, tell me about you."

VERA, 31, ANNAPOLIS, MD.

Tanya told me that she was the best thing that could ever happen to me. She said this about thirty times, in case repeating it would make me believe it. Actually, she has me thinking about it.

ROY, 44, CLEVELAND, OHIO

★★★★★★★★★★★★★

Paul talked military. When I told him anything significant, he nodded and said, "I copy." He told the waiter to "stand by" while we read the menu, and called the men's room the "latrine." When I asked him to get my coat, he replied, "Roger, wilco."

ELLEN, 27, DENVER, COLO.

★★★★★★★★★★★★★ 75

He did imitations. The whole night. Every time he talked, he "did" somebody else: James Cagney, Cary Grant, Ronald Reagan, Jerry Seinfeld, Jim Carrey. Burt Lancaster. Some rapper. I have no idea who *he* is. Or what his own voice sounds like.

ELAINE, 31, DENVER, COLO.

★★★★★★★★★★★★★

She worried about everything. If she looked okay, if her hair looked good. If she was dressed right. If she was too late. If we'd be on time. If there was too much traffic. If I was driving too fast. If they'd hold the reservation. If the meat would be too rare, if she'd ordered too much, if I was spending too much, if she was getting fat. During dinner she worried about the ozone layer, the gorillas, the situation in Iraq. She worried that, while we were eating dinner, rain forests were being chopped or burned down. She even worried that she was worrying too much and spoiling our date.

MEL, 41, SAN FRANCISCO, CALIF.

★ ★ ★ ★ ★ ★ ★ ★ ★ ★ ★ ★ ★ **77**

This is what he told me on our date: His eyes bother him and his arthritis. His teeth are a pain. He has bursitis and a bad knee, and he had open-heart surgery a year ago. He also can't hear. He told me all this several times; apparently he also can't remember.

BETTY, 62, NEW YORK, N.Y.

Ned told me he was shy and kept referring to a list he'd made of topics to talk about and jokes to tell.

IRIS, 20, SYRACUSE, N.Y.

★ ★ ★ ★ ★ ★ ★ ★ ★ ★ ★ ★ ★

Everything that happened, he put up his hand and said, "Slap me five." We get a parking space: Slap me five. We get seated at the restaurant without waiting: Slap me five. I like the egg roll: Slap me five. By the end of the evening, I wanted to slap him silly.

SKYLAR, 22, SILVER SPRING, MD.

★ ★ ★ ★ ★ ★ ★ ★ ★ ★ ★ ★ ★ ★ 79

I know that Louise is older than I am, and I'm not sure how she feels about it. So I told her that I'm five years older than I really am. She probably told me that she's ten years younger.

SETH, 23, WICHITA, KANS.

He interrupted me every time I opened my mouth. Assumed he knew the end of my sentences. Gradually, I stopped talking. No matter, he conducted both parts of the conversation.

JILL, 42, PHOENIX, ARIZ.

★★★★★★★★★★★★★

Over dinner, getting acquainted, he told me that his best friend had just committed suicide. Then he mentioned that his girlfriend had just left him and, by the way, she was pregnant with his baby. Before I knew it, he was crying, tears streaming down his cheeks. He said he was afraid of getting cancer. He didn't think he'd live a long life. He soaked his napkin and blew his nose into the tablecloth. Then he wiped his eyes and asked me if I'd like to go out again on Sunday.

MARY, 28, NEW YORK, N.Y.

★ ★ ★ ★ ★ ★ ★ ★ ★ ★ ★ ★ ★ ★

Toward the end of the evening, I'm thinking that this guy's really kind of sexy, that he has a really nice set of lips. That I'd really like to kiss them. I'm leaning his way, staring up into his eyes, and he meets my eyes and talks about how much money his new computer system is saving him. Oh well.

SANDIE, 25, DUBUQUE, IOWA

★★★★★★★★★★★★★

Sherrie talked constantly—while riding, while watching the movie, while chewing her pizza. I finally got her to shut up by kissing her, but she waited until we took a breather and picked up her monologue exactly where she left off. At the very *word*.

SCOTT, 25, INDIANAPOLIS, IND.

Apparently, Alice thought that a date was an occasion to discuss the details of her failed marriage. And much cheaper than a shrink.

BRUCE, 44, WILMINGTON, DEL.

★★★★★★★★★★★★★

Sonia took me to a family dinner. Her aunt kept pushing food at me, and she fussed until I ate it. I thought she was going to spoon it into my mouth. Everyone spoke Hungarian. They'd look at me and nod and talk, laugh out loud. Howl with laughter. I sort of smiled. I had no idea the whole night what was going on.

JASON, 30, WASHINGTON, D.C.

★ ★ ★ ★ ★ ★ ★ ★ ★ ★ ★ ★ ★

All night, he talked about his mother. How perfect she is. How her arthritis bothers her but she never complains. How she's the most intelligent woman he's ever met, a perfect lady, a wonderful hostess, mother, cook, homemaker. Beautiful. Poised. Witty. He said, age aside, that if she weren't his mother, he'd want to marry her, and he excused himself at nine o'clock so he could call her to say good night.

EBONY, 29, SAN FRANCISCO, CALIF.

★ ★ ★ ★ ★ ★ ★ ★ ★ ★ ★ ★ ★

At the end of the evening, Yvonne knew nothing about me. And, actually, I knew nothing about her. But I knew more than I'd ever want to about her flawless former boyfriend, Edmond, against whom no man can compete.

BERT, 38, NEW YORK, N.Y.

He told me he had been a women's studies major at the same university I'd gone to. On our second date, I learned that he never graduated. But he hadn't exactly *lied*; in actual fact, he'd hung around campus, studying women.

PAULA, 22, CORAL GABLES, FLA.

86 ★★★★★★★★★★★★★★

Brad told me I was the most beautiful woman he'd ever seen. He ogled me. Whatever I said, he agreed. Whatever I liked, he liked. Whatever opinions I had, he shared. He was like a parrot. "Ice skating? I love it too." "Anchovies? Nothing better." Finally, I began to tell him I liked things I actually can't stand. Professional wrestling. Bluefish. Line dancing. He said he liked all that too. I'd had it. I told him he was a fool. He nodded, held my hand, and asked if I believed in love at first sight.

SARAH, 31, SAN ANTONIO, TEX.

★ ★ ★ ★ ★ ★ ★ ★ ★ ★ ★ ★

Frank kept calling me "Charlene." He said I looked like a Charlene. I bet Charlene and I don't look alike; probably the only thing we have in common is that we're both unfortunate enough to have gone out with Frank.

LIZ, 32, CAMDEN, MAINE

"Lois, huh?" He kept saying that. "Lois, huh? I've never been out with a 'Lois' before." Like what? Each name is a different breed?

LOIS, 30, ST. LOUIS, MO.

Liz complimented me about everything. She told me I dress great and I've got great taste. She said I'm intelligent, fascinating, and clever. Also, thoughtful and generous, and I have penetrating eyes and strong features. According to her, I'm pretty fantastic. I can't wait to take her out again. She's incredibly perceptive.

PAUL, 33, BATON ROUGE, LA.

★ ★ ★ ★ ★ ★ ★ ★ ★ ★ ★ ★ ★ ★ 89

Jesse bragged that I was the first woman of his race or religion he'd been out with since high school. Like I should be honored.

GABRIELLA, 23, NILES, ILL.

I asked him not to smoke. "Why?" he said. "Is it a crime?"

I said smoke bothered me. He said, "Oh, you're not one of those picky, high-maintenance broads, are you?" That ended the conversation. Not to mention the evening.

ILANA, 26, ATLANTA, GA.

★★★★★★★★★★★★★

He found out my age, looked me over, and said, "You don't look so bad for thirty." He thought this was a compliment.

MARGO, 32, INDIANAPOLIS, IND.

She came dressed all in tie-dye. A hippie. Rings on every finger. Like that. She said she admired my aura. That it was rare to see a man with a sky blue–pink aura. She just *had* to experience me. To mingle our auras would add to the harmony of the planet. I thought she was nuts, but I didn't argue with her, no sir. Mingling auras sounded like it might just be fun.

DIGGER, 41, TAOS, N.MEX.

★ ★ ★ ★ ★ ★ ★ ★ ★ ★ ★ ★ ★ ★ ★ 91

He sat across the table, looked into my eyes, and compared me to his old girlfriend. My eyes were almost as blue, my hair not quite as full. My lips a bit fuller. But all in all, despite the differences, I was attractive, in my own way. Still, she knew him much better, better than anyone had ever known him, and she had this mysterious, charismatic quality that I lacked.

DODIE, 29, CLEVELAND, OHIO

Leonard couldn't stop talking. He talked the whole night. I didn't get a word in. When he pulled up to my building to drop me off, he kept on talking. I couldn't break in to thank him or say good night, so I just opened the door to get out. He kept talking.

I put my foot out onto the curb; he kept talking. I got out, closed the door; he opened his window and leaned his head out, still talking. I heard his voice trailing after me until I closed the front door.

VANESSA, 31, CLEVELAND, OHIO

★ ★ ★ ★ ★ ★ ★ ★ ★ ★ ★ ★ ★

CHAPTER THREE

★ The Food ★ of Love

As long as anyone can remember, good food and drink have gone hand in hand with good conversation, good company, and good cheer. Meals are basic and comforting; eating is primal and sensual. So naturally, when dining is done on a date, it tends to bring down barriers and build up bonds, reduce inhibitions and encourage intimacies. And that is why—whether candlelit in cafés or home-cooked in kitchens, savored at sunset or delivered at dawn, set with silver on a table or spread on a blanket on the lawn—meals provide the backdrop for countless dates. And perfect opportunities for dates to test each other's taste and table manners.

"Stanley used his fork like a shovel," Marianne recalls. "His face was an inch above his plate, and his fork moved back and forth between the two. His meal was gone before mine had cooled enough to taste."

While many romances begin at cocktails or dinner, many others bite the dust there. Like any

other dating activity, dining has its perils and pitfalls. And many a relationship has been broken along with the bread.

★ ★ ★ ★ ★ ★ ★ ★ ★ ★ ★ ★ ★

Carolyn stood at the door of the restaurant and waited in the cold for me to open the door for her. She could not bring herself to open the door. She stood at the table and waited for me to pull out her chair. After she went to the ladies' room, she stood waiting for me to get up and seat her. This got old quickly.

RANDY, 31, BRAINTREE, MASS.

★★★★★★★★★★★★★

Irene is a fanatic vegetarian. So I pretended I was too. Now that we're dating, all I can eat when I'm with her is tofu, sprouts, and beans.

SAL, 29, SAN ANTONIO, TEX.

Janie weighs maybe a hundred pounds. She's about five foot two. I have never, and I mean never, seen somebody eat as much as she did. Before dinner, she said she could eat her own weight in red meat, and I believed her. I kept hoping the meal would arrive. I didn't like the way she was looking at me.

MEL, 40, TULSA, OKLA.

★ ★ ★ ★ ★ ★ ★ ★ ★ ★ ★ ★ ★ ★ ★

Arnold took ten minutes to sample the wine. He sniffed it, held his breath, and his eyes rolled back in his head. Then he sipped it and rolled it around on his tongue with his eyes closed. He twisted his mouth, splashed it around from cheek to cheek, like mouthwash. His face looked like he was in pain. Finally, he swallowed and, still with his eyes closed, he nodded. The waiter filled my glass. By the time Arnold opened his eyes, I'd drained it.

CHLOE, 28, STAMFORD, CONN.

★ ★ ★ ★ ★ ★ ★ ★ ★ ★ ★ ★ ★ ★

Anna gave me a sip of her black Russian. From her mouth. I wasn't expecting it and pulled away; it dribbled down her face, all over her dress, my shirt, the tablecloth.

ERIC, 25, DENVER, COLO.

It's our first date. Bernard takes me to an expensive restaurant and, as I'm sipping my soup, he takes out two condoms, lays them beside his plate, and says he's saving them for dessert.

BRIDGET, 48, KISSIMMEE, FLA.

★ ★ ★ ★ ★ ★ ★ ★ ★ ★ ★ ★ ★ ★ *101*

I have never seen anyone eat as slowly as Monica. I took her to lunch. It took her an hour and a half to finish a bowl of soup. By the time she finished her sandwich, my butt had gone numb from sitting and I was hungry for dinner.

AL, 32, CHARLOTTE, N.C.

★★★★★★★★★★★★★

A herd of goats died to make her dining room table. She bragged that it was laminated goat skin. On this table of death, she served blood-red filet. And she bragged that the huge mirror on the wall was framed in whale bones. I felt like I was in a house of horrors.

BERT, 47, YARDLEY, PA.

★★★★★★★★★★★★★★ 103

Vanessa offered to cook for me and proceeded to fight, I mean physically *fight,* with her appliances. She burned a finger on the toaster oven and told it that it was in big trouble and pulled out the plug. When the vegetable drawer got stuck, she battled with it—tugged, pushed, slammed, arguing with it the whole time. If I hadn't stepped in, she'd have trashed it. Maybe she was nervous about dinner, but she *talked* to her dishwasher and scolded her stove when the flame was too high, as if she had no concept of inanimate objects.

KEVIN, 23, SAVANNAH, GA.

★ ★ ★ ★ ★ ★ ★ ★ ★ ★ ★ ★ ★

Pam suggested that we "share" dessert, a piece of apple pie à la mode. I managed to dive in once, while she was chewing, and I got a taste of ice cream with a little bit of crust. But the way she attacked that plate, I was afraid to try for more. Truly, her fork was a weapon. It was dangerous to get between Pam and her pie.

DENNIS, 42, TAMPA, FLA.

★★★★★★★★★★★★★★

I was fixed up with Latrice. I took her to dinner. All she would eat was a small green salad with oil and vinegar. Not a large green salad, a small one. Not a piece of bread. I felt guilty ordering a regular meal. I offered her a piece of my filet, some of my potato. She sat and watched me eat, nibbled an occasional shredded radish. It was like feasting in front of a poster child for some famine relief organization.

JIMMY, 32, CLEVELAND, OHIO

Mitch ordered one entrée. "They're big," he said. "We can share."

CAMILLE, BIRMINGHAM, ALA.

106 ★ ★ ★ ★ ★ ★ ★ ★ ★ ★ ★ ★ ★

As we dined, Lori rubbed my leg under the table, playing footsie. We drank champagne. She ran her tongue across her lips and told me how the bubbles made her lips tingle. I leaned across to see for myself and knocked over the champagne bucket. The entire thing—ice, bottle, champagne—all clattered to the floor. Heads turned, people stared. So much for "the moment."

MATT, 23, BOULDER, COLO.

Alexis talked with her mouth full. When she was animated, bits of food flew from her lips and landed all over the table.

GREG, 55, CHICAGO, ILL.

★ ★ ★ ★ ★ ★ ★ ★ ★ ★ ★ ★ ★ ★ **107**

I was dating Daniel and ending a year long relationship with Greg. Daniel's family was coming to town. He wanted me to meet them, so I offered to cook dinner. Unfortunately, their flight was delayed. Daniel came over to tell me, but I was out grocery shopping so he left a note in my mailbox. I'd already picked up the mail, so I never got the note. I made dinner. Nobody showed up. I was furious. I called Greg and made a date for the next night. I couldn't believe Daniel had stood me up. The next night, Sunday, when I was entertaining Greg, who knocks at the door expecting dinner? Daniel, his mother, and his father. Apparently, his note said they were coming in late Saturday night and asked me to change the dinner date to Sunday, to call him if it wasn't okay. I invited them in and offered them some of our wine. It was awful.

DEBRA, 23, PALO ALTO, CALIF.

★★★★★★★★★★★★★

I bought Sondra lunch and she lost a tooth in her hoagie. It shattered or something. Not a pretty sight.

BEN, 41, DOVER, DEL.

Greg took me to dinner and then cited the amount and types of fat and cholesterol in my prime rib. He was like a walking list of nutritional information. To him, food was a plateful of chemical components—fiber, fat, minerals, complex and simple carbohydrates. It got so I didn't even want to touch my meal, much less swallow it.

MELANIE, 39, KANSAS CITY, MO.

★★★★★★★★★★★★★★ 109

George stared at me all through dinner—so intensely that it was scary. He was so *focused*. Then, all of a sudden, splat—he plopped forward, smack into his enchiladas. I thought, "Ohmygosh, he's dead!" And he was—dead drunk. When the waiter sat him up, there were refried beans hanging from his nose and his glasses were still in the enchiladas.

FAYE, 27, BOULDER, COLO.

I cut the pasta. I didn't roll it. You'd have thought I'd smashed his car.

GERI, 28, SAGINAW, MICH.

She couldn't stop talking, even when she was pouring coffee. She was looking at me, gabbing, altogether missed the mug, and managed to pour my coffee all over me. I thought the skin would peel right off my thighs.

JORDAN, 28, ST. PAUL, MINN.

★★★★★★★★★★★★★★ 111

Maria would not talk directly to the waiter. She told me what she wanted and expected me to tell him. "I'll have lentil soup." "She'll have lentil soup." "And the duckling." "And the duckling." "No, change the soup to house salad." It was ridiculous. I felt like a parrot. Or like I was playing that kids' game, passing the message down the line.

JEROME, 31, BALTIMORE, MD.

★ ★ ★ ★ ★ ★ ★ ★ ★ ★ ★ ★ ★ ★

I asked David in for coffee. Little did I know he'd lecture me about the inferiority of instant. The decadence of decaf. We're talking serious coffee snob, here. To him, my coffee was a character flaw.

SAMANTHA, 23, ANN ARBOR, MICH.

All during dinner, Randy talked about his heart surgery. Details of the process, the anesthesia, the recovery. Right at the table, he opened his shirt to show me the scar. At least it wasn't hemorrhoid surgery.

MARIE, 39, MARION, OHIO

★ ★ ★ ★ ★ ★ ★ ★ ★ ★ ★ ★ ★ ★

Jasmine ordered a steak. Somehow, she managed to cut it so fiercely that it went flying off her plate, across the table, and onto the floor. Just as a couple was being escorted to their table. The woman tripped on the steak and went down screaming. Everyone in the restaurant was staring. Jasmine wasn't the least bit rattled. She wanted a new steak and said the old one was tough.

TYRONE, 24, WASHINGTON, D.C.

★ ★ ★ ★ ★ ★ ★ ★ ★ ★ ★ ★ ★

I ordered veal and all through dinner, he wouldn't stop talking about how I was eating a dead animal. How my dinner used to have a face.

MARGE, 31, DENVER, COLO.

Constance ordered in French in French restaurants and in Italian in Italian restaurants. When we went for Mexican food, she ordered in Spanish. And none of the waiters, in any of these restaurants, could understand a word she said.

HARRIS, 33, NEW YORK, N.Y.

He chewed out the waiter for bringing his steak too well done. Asked him if he was hard of hearing or just stupid. Demanded "consideration" from the manager, in the form of free drinks, and then he didn't leave a tip.

JOAN, 43, BOSTON, MASS.

★ ★ ★ ★ ★ ★ ★ ★ ★ ★ ★ ★ ★

We'd had a long, romantic dinner and a couple bottles of wine. When we got to my car, I asked Laura if she wanted to go back to my place. She nodded and leaned against the car, a dreamy look on her face, and looked up at me. I leaned over to kiss her and, just as I did, she slid—no, it was more of a plop—down between my arms right onto the ground. Her head rested on my hubcap. She was sound asleep. Passed out. Snoring. I had to drag her to the car door, lift her into the seat, and deposit her at her apartment. She didn't wake up the whole time.

LOWELL, 30, BROOKLINE, MASS.

★ ★ ★ ★ ★ ★ ★ ★ ★ ★ ★ ★ ★ 117

Whitney thought the people at the next table were eavesdropping, so she said outrageous things, just to shock them. She told me not to chicken out; no one would ever suspect us. We had to kill the creep, like we'd talked about. When they got really silent and leaned toward us, trying to hear more, she began talking pig-Latin. "Omebody-say as-hay ig-bay ose-nay."

DAVE, 31, AMHERST, MASS.

On our first date, for brunch, he licked a strawberry and said he'd love to suck my toes.

SHELLEY, 29, SEATTLE, WASH.

★ ★ ★ ★ ★ ★ ★ ★ ★ ★ ★ ★ ★ ★

Avery called me every night for two weeks, asking me to have dinner with him. Finally I went. He took me to McDonald's. As he chowed down on his Quarter Pounder, he asked me if I could get him fixed up with my sister.

GWEN, 23, BROOKLINE, MASS.

★★★★★★★★★★★★★★

To impress David, I invited him to dinner at my sorority house. Tables were set up all over, since everyone had dates. As I carried our tray through the foyer, I looked up and smiled at David, slipped on a piece of ice and fell on my butt, my legs spread in opposite directions. Lamb chops flew across the room. Applesauce splattered the wall. Corn was everywhere. David was impressed.

JANIE, 20, ITHACA, N.Y.

He spent our whole dinner talking on his portable phone. His office, his broker, his client, his four-year-old son, his ex-wife. I entertained myself by ordering more food and drinks. Had two desserts. Finally, sitting across the table, I called him from *my* portable. He laughed and said he'd get back to me.

ANGIE, 33, CORAL GABLES, FLA.

★★★★★★★★★★★★★★ 121

CHAPTER FOUR

★ Fun Times ★

I n the process of getting to know each other, couples try to have fun. One partner's concept of "fun," however, might differ from the other's. If, for fun, Joe does demolition derbies and Jane does découpage, their enjoyment of their dates might dwindle.

Common interests can make or break relationships, but often, couples don't initially share them. Some introduce their partners to their passions. "Brad said I'd love fishing," Tracey recalls. "So I got up at four A.M. to be offshore by dawn. Half asleep, I watched him catch a dozen bluefish. He showed me how to clean and gut them. Fish tissue and blood all over the deck, all over *me*. He thought it was wonderful."

Other couples explore new activities together, with varying degrees of success. "We signed up for ballroom dancing," Stan says. "We thought it would be 'our thing.' But Kathy kicked when she should have dipped, and I was a soprano for the rest of the weekend. So we signed up for bridge lessons. Kathy fell asleep at the second class. Next, I think we'll try a movie."

Some who have no luck finding mutual "fun" remain drawn to each other anyway, going their

124

separate ways for "fun" and meeting afterward. Sharon explains, "Ed and I stay together *only* because we have an agreement: I don't make him garden and he doesn't make me bowl."

If nothing else, couples learn a lot about each other by their ideas of fun. And sometimes, even if the relationship doesn't work out, the activity does; long after Joe has Jane, he'll still have découpage.

★ ★ ★ ★ ★ ★ ★ ★ ★ ★ ★ ★ ★

He's a dentist, and he collects old dentistry equipment. All over his house, like works of art. I don't mean just old chairs and skinny little drawers. He has mirrors, the pliers, picks, hammers, and he loves to show them to you, discuss how they were used—it reminded me of a torture chamber.

LENORE, 33, BOSTON, MASS.

★★★★★★★★★★★★★

He took me home to show me his butterfly collection. Hundreds, thousands of dead bugs pinned to the walls, all over the house. Even in the powder room. Everywhere. I've had *nightmares* about that place.

ANNE, 26, SAN FRANCISCO, CALIF.

He brought me to a party. Everyone was stark naked. Before I could close my mouth, he'd shed his shirt, dropped his trousers, and plopped into the hot tub, from which he told me how I'd be much less conspicuous if I disrobed.

DEBBIE, 34, LOS ANGELES, CALIF.

★ ★ ★ ★ ★ ★ ★ ★ ★ ★ ★ ★ ★ ★ ★ 127

Raymond took me to a party, offered me marijuana, and started licking my shoulder.

VIRGINIA, 21, CASPER, WYO.

Every day, at work, I'd see Ted in conservative business suits. But when he showed up for a date, I almost didn't recognize him. He had his hair slicked back and wore a nylon shirt, unbuttoned halfway down his chest to show off his chest hair. And gold chains, half a dozen of them, around his neck. Polyester everything. His *real* self. A regular party animal. From the seventies.

CELIA, ST. LOUIS, MO.

★ ★ ★ ★ ★ ★ ★ ★ ★ ★ ★ ★ ★

I had a blind date for my sorority's fall hayride. We had to take a long ride on a schoolbus to get to the stables. It was crowded, so the girls all sat on their dates' laps. My date promptly proceeded to throw up all over the back of the new one-hundred-dollar sweater I'd bought for this event. He claimed it was something he ate, but he didn't need to tell *me* that—I was well aware of what he'd eaten. I was wearing a nasty combination of a sausage pizza and beer.

CORRIE, 22, COLUMBIA, MO.

We spent the weekend doing his errands—his grocery shopping, laundry, his fixing up and cleaning up. When I got home, *my* grocery list, laundry, and cleaning were waiting to greet me. Of course, he couldn't stay to help; he needed time to relax.

GWEN, 39, HILTON HEAD, S.C.

Leo never made plans. He'd show up. But he had no ideas about what to do next. It was like, "Here I am, what are you going to do with me?"

ADELLE, 30, BROOKLINE, MASS.

Morris arrived and sat. He wouldn't budge. He sat on my sofa and watched TV. Sometimes he'd ask for a beer or a soft drink. At first, I waited for him to get up and tell me where we were going. But he never did. And, when he was leaving, he'd say, "I'm glad you didn't want to go out. It's much nicer staying in."

EVELYN, 66, CHICAGO, ILL.

★★★★★★★★★★★★★★★ 131

Every weekend, Walter brought his laundry to my place. His laundry room is in the basement of his building. He said he'd rather wash in a machine where he knows who else uses it. He used my bleach and my detergent. I spent Saturday nights folding his shorts.

APRIL, 37, NEW YORK, N.Y.

He thought it would be fun to get my parakeet drunk and poured vodka into its water. The next day it was dead. He denies this ever happened.

GAIL, 30, RENO, NEV.

★★★★★★★★★★★★★★★

I was invited to my office's fiftieth anniversary. I brought Les as my date. Everyone from work was there—the owners of the company, my boss, *his* boss. And Les loved the band so much, he took it upon himself to start break-dancing. It caught everyone's eye. The party stopped; everyone watched him. I tried to leave quietly, as if I had no idea who he was, but of course, he had the keys to the car.

JASMINE, 21, CLEVELAND, OHIO

With Nick, it's never just a date. It's parasailing, deep-sea fishing, soaring, snorkeling, hiking. I long to sack out beside a TV and munch a pizza. But he thinks I'm his soul mate; I don't dare tell him.

FAITH, 22, MIAMI, FLA.

The woman could not dance. She had absolutely no rhythm, couldn't follow my lead, nothing. None. It was like she was stomping out a fire. Or killing army ants. I had to move away or get hurt.

KENNETH, 31, DARIEN, CONN.

He was a great dancer and I was having a blast. Until I ran my hand through his hair and he ran, screaming, literally howling, off the dance floor. He was gone, in the men's room for about twenty minutes. When he came back, he told me never, never under any circumstances to touch his hair. Trust me . . .

DONNA, 34, CHERRY HILL, N.J.

★ ★ ★ ★ ★ ★ ★ ★ ★ ★ ★ ★ ★ ★ **135**

It was snowing pretty bad, so her parents suggested I spend the night in the guest room. As I was going to bed, they said, "By the way, Blossom's loose—Don't be surprised if you see her." I figured Blossom was a rabbit or a hamster, since I'd seen a cage in the family room. I'm asleep. I dream something very long and slithery is sliding up my leg onto my belly. A python? A boa? Some very large snake. Suddenly, I open my eyes and realize I'm not dreaming. I fly out of bed, run screaming down the hall. I'm sputtering, unable to make words. My date, her parents, and her sisters come out of their rooms. That's when I realize I'm standing there stark naked. Her dad grins and says, "Well, what do you know? I guess he found Blossom."

STEVE, 24, TWIN FALLS, IDAHO

★ ★ ★ ★ ★ ★ ★ ★ ★ ★ ★ ★ ★

We were in the mall. They pipe in music. Gary grabs me and starts dancing around the floor, waltzing. Kill me, I think. Somebody just kill me now.

ERICA, 21, SPRINGFIELD, PA.

Waiting in line for tickets to a show, Brendan starts dancing. There's no music, no reason. He just dances in place, a little two-step. I think, does he have to go to the bathroom? Does anyone notice this but me? Is he dangerous?

LINDA, 30, PHILADELPHIA, PA.

★ ★ ★ ★ ★ ★ ★ ★ ★ ★ ★ ★ ★ ★ 137

Dave asked me over for dinner. When I got there, he told me to "make myself at home," and then he pumped iron in the basement for an hour. After that he took a shower. It was like he didn't know I was there. I didn't get upset; I made long-distance calls. At least, when the bills come, he'll know.

DENA, 34, CHICAGO, ILL.

★ ★ ★ ★ ★ ★ ★ ★ ★ ★ ★ ★ ★

He likes to go bar-hopping. And it seems like, every bar we go to, the waitresses know him. Know him *well*.

LOIS, 31, NASHVILLE, TENN.

After our first date, Trevor called my phone machine six or seven times a day with messages about what a good time he'd had, how he couldn't wait to see me again, how attractive he found me, how he couldn't get anything done because he was thinking about me, imagining our next time together. Gag me.

GIGI, 22, STARKVILLE, MISS.

★ ★ ★ ★ ★ ★ ★ ★ ★ ★ ★ ★ ★ ★ ★ 139

As soon as Steve showed up, my phone rang. It was for him. The guy calling sounded like a thug. Steve apologized and said he'd given my phone number to his dispatcher, in case anyone needed him. He took the call and, as we started to leave, he got another. For about two weeks, he continued getting calls at my number. And some guy kept calling because he didn't believe me when I said Steve wasn't there and wasn't going to be, either. He called about four times in a half hour and said, "When you see him, you tell him to call me." It was scary.

EVA, 31, ATLANTA, GA.

Maureen has about forty locks on her door. You spend forty minutes getting in and another forty relocking them from the inside. When you want to leave, it takes forty for her to unlock them to let you out. That's basically how we spent the evening.

MARC, 23, NEW YORK, N.Y.

★ ★ ★ ★ ★ ★ ★ ★ ★ ★ ★ ★ ★ 141

Faye had lists of everything. She had them with her—a list for the supermarket, a list of chores, a list of people to call, a list of bills to pay. She even had a list of what she had to do that day, including our date—a schedule. And she checked items off one by one as we did them. Get picked up at 7:00. Check. Movie, 7:20. Check. At the door, we kissed, and I reminded her to check it off the list.

WILLIAM, 43, LANCASTER, PA.

★ ★ ★ ★ ★ ★ ★ ★ ★ ★ ★ ★ ★

Gary requires equipment for everything he does. If we go for a hike, he needs to dress in mountain boots and carry a survival kit. He packs a pocketknife, sunscreen, bug spray, a water bottle, a jacket, candy bars, a first-aid kit, a flare gun, a camera, a phone—and *that's* just to walk through the park.

EDEN, 40, VALLEY FORGE, PA.

Tom said he had shelves full of porno tapes. Instead of going out, he wanted to stay home and watch them. He also wanted to make our own.

HEATHER, 30, ALBUQUERQUE, N.MEX.

★ ★ ★ ★ ★ ★ ★ ★ ★ ★ ★ ★ ★ ★ ★ 143

Paul videotapes everything. Everyplace we go, he takes the damn videocam, and extra batteries and cassettes. But he doesn't just tape places. If I want to discuss something important—like our relationship— he tells me to wait till he checks the sound levels, and to talk directly to the lens. He says he's working on a documentary of his life.

CASEY, 19, SELMA, ALA.

144 ★★★★★★★★★★★★★★

An evening with Missy is a talk-show marathon. She works all day, so she tapes the shows and watches them at night. That's all she wants to do. She talks about TV personalities as if they're her personal friends. She quotes Oprah and Montel, has a gripe with Sally. She adores Jerry, thinks he's a peach.

ALEC, 41, MILWAUKEE, WIS.

We played strip poker. I'm sitting there butt naked; she's taken off her watch. This was not what I'd had in mind.

PATRICK, 22, FORT LAUDERDALE, FLA.

★★★★★★★★★★★★★★ 145

I wanted to impress John that I was the perfect mate for him—that I could manage his home, that I was competent, efficient, and intelligent. But he had an electric stove, so there were no flames. When I made dinner, I didn't remember to turn off the burner and, ever so casually, holding a wine glass in my left hand, I leaned my right hand flat on the burner. You could hear the sizzle. I was too embarrassed to scream in front of John. I twisted a smile, made light of my mistake. And kept my hand slathered in aloe for the next three days.

SUE, 26, NEW YORK, N.Y.

★★★★★★★★★★★★★

Mark became possessed when we watched football. He couldn't just watch the game; he'd suddenly be on his feet—not just cheering, but yelling, screaming, jumping, cursing. He'd wave his arms, gesture, bang, pound, throw things. Then, just as suddenly, he'd sit down, like nothing had happened.

GLORIA, 39, WILMINGTON, DEL.

★★★★★★★★★★★★★★

Pete asked me out. He took me to his couch. In front of the TV. "Isn't this great? Everything I need's right here. Beer, the NBA, and thou. You can have your Vegas nights and Broadway lights. We're sitting on the best place on earth."

DANA, 28, BROOKLYN, N.Y.

I couldn't hear the movie. All I could hear was James smacking his lips and crunching his popcorn. Smack smack crunch crunch. Occasionally, a slurp of soda—which he finished, and then he sucked air through the straw.

SAMANTHA, 22, FORT WORTH, TEX.

He chose the movie, but he talked the entire time—about nothing. People were going, "Shh," and giving him dirty looks, but he kept talking, and not even about things that pertained to the plot or the scenery. He talked about what time it was, where he'd eaten lunch that day, his softball team. When the movie was over, I asked him if he'd enjoyed it. He said it was great, but I doubt he had a clue.

TONI, 23, SAN FRANCISCO, CALIF.

★★★★★★★★★★★★★★ 149

We went to a movie. Alec broke up laughing, I mean *guffawing,* at *nothing.* Maybe he had a private joke that he alone could enjoy. But he laughed out loud, slapped his knee, doubled over. Maybe he was stoned? I don't know. I never asked.

GENA, 40, FORT WASHINGTON, PA.

★★★★★★★★★★★★★★

Tamara cried through the whole show. I mean, she *cried*. Sobbed. I asked if she wanted to leave, go someplace else, go home. She apologized and said no, she was fine. But I could hear her, sniffling through the whole movie. Afterward, I told her to cheer up. It was sad, but it was a *movie*. She got mad at me. Like I must be a completely insensitive brute because I didn't weep.

JEFF, 31, FORT WORTH, TEX.

★★★★★★★★★★★★★★★ *151*

I'm the guy who took the girl to the movie where she dropped her contact lens. No kidding. The whole bit. Hunting under the seats, reaching into stuff mortal men fear to touch, fingering the soda and popcorn and sticky stuff you don't want to think about in search of her contact lens, which of course we never found. What was she taking it out for in the dark anyway?

STAN, 30, DARIEN, CONN.

We went to the shore. I was sunbathing, unhooked my top to tan my back, and dozed off in the sun. Suddenly, cold water splashes on my back and I sit up startled, forgetting my bra. Mitch grins and says, "Oh, hello." He's, of course, talking to my chest.

BEVERLY, 26, WILMINGTON, DEL.

★★★★★★★★★★★★★★ 153

We went to see *Dracula* at a horror film festival. Tina sank down in her chair and hid behind her hands. When they got ready to drive the stake through the vampire's heart, Tina bolted out of her seat and ran out of the theater. I was telling her, "Tina, it's only a *movie*." But she was outta there.

SEBASTIAN, 26, SALINA, KANS.

Joe's idea of a good time was having me watch him play video games at an arcade.

KATIE, 33, KANSAS CITY, MO.

★ ★ ★ ★ ★ ★ ★ ★ ★ ★ ★ ★ ★

I take Sally to the movies and buy her a large popcorn. I hand it to her and she spills it. The container falls right through her hands. So I go get back in line, wait, and buy her another. I get back into my seat and hand it to her, but I trip over some guy's feet and this time *I* drop the popcorn. By this time, we're ankle-deep in popcorn and the movie's been going for about fifteen minutes. But I'm determined. I go back, wait in the line again, and ten minutes later, having missed half an hour of the movie, I come back with the popcorn. She won't eat it. It seems she doesn't like it buttered.

MIKE, 28, LEXINGTON, KY.

★ ★ ★ ★ ★ ★ ★ ★ ★ ★ ★ ★ ★ 155

I told her that I burn easily. It was a good way to get her to rub sunblock on my back—and all the other places I can't reach. And, of course, I need several coats of it, given my fair complexion. I guess I'll say or do almost anything to get a back rub.

SEAN, 23, CONCORD, N.H.

We drove to the ocean. She wanted to take my picture on the boardwalk. She got the camera focused on me, and she backed up to get her shot. I tried to warn her, but she stepped back anyhow and got hit by a bike. Meantime, in the confusion, her camera was sitting on the ground and somebody stole it. Her leg swelled up like a football. And, as if that wasn't enough, it started to rain.

MIKE, 24, NEWARK, DEL.

★ ★ ★ ★ ★ ★ ★ ★ ★ ★ ★ ★ ★ ★

First date, Paul and I go to the zoo. It must be mating season. Everywhere we look, the animals are having sex. The giant tortoises are humping so slowly, the males groaning so loud, you think you should call a vet. The monkeys and chimpanzees are all banging away. It was like walking through a porno shop. I'm trying to find something else to talk about, but no. Paul thinks it's great. He points out one chimp who's not having sex. He's ignoring his mate and playing with himself—masturbating. I feel my skin turn bright red. I'm embarrassed. Paul says, "Poor guy. I've had dates like that. He got stuck with an ugly one."

MAUREEN, 25, SAN DIEGO, CALIF.

★ ★ ★ ★ ★ ★ ★ ★ ★ ★ ★ ★ ★

I took her to a karaoke bar. She wouldn't get off stage. Other people wanted a turn, but she wouldn't surrender. They got her off for one number, a guy. Then she went back on stage and joined him. They needed the hook.

PETER, 50, MEDFORD, N.J.

We spent a day at the beach. All Faith wanted to do was get a tan. No swimming, no surfing, no volleyball. No snorkeling. No windsurfing. The woman would not even walk around looking for shells. I couldn't even sit next to her to talk; I was "blocking the rays." Of course, on the way home, she was sulking because she got burned.

JOE, 30, TOMS RIVER, N.J.

Todd did magic tricks. He tried to impress me by taking quarters out of my nose. I thought he was getting romantic; he was taking a jack of hearts out of my blouse.

SOPHIE, 21, SACRAMENTO, CALIF.

160 ★ ★ ★ ★ ★ ★ ★ ★ ★ ★ ★ ★

It was a beautiful day in April. We drove to the shore. I parked my sports utility vehicle on the beach and we got out to walk along the water. When we got back, the tide had come in and my vehicle had sunk to the hubcaps in the sand. It took the rest of the day to get help, because the beach was basically deserted, and the year-round residents I asked for help just came down to the beach and gawked, chuckling to them-selves about the big-city jerk who got his fancy vehicle stuck in the sand. Let's just say that things did not go as I'd planned.

TED, 42, WAYNE, PA.

★ ★ ★ ★ ★ ★ ★ ★ ★ ★ ★ ★ ★

Bob's a gambler. He'll bet on anything. Not just at the casino or at cards; he bets on sports. He bets on horses. He bets on who will win an election, which way a jury will decide, who'll get the most french fries, whether a coin will land heads up or down, whether or not he can break his record of nine orgasms in a day. And he is not a good loser.

SAMMY, 27, CAPE MAY, N.J.

★★★★★★★★★★★★★

Dave and I met in Shakespeare class. All night, he kept slipping in and out of characters from the plays we were studying, quoting lines. He looked into my eyes and whispered, "Rose, Rose, Rose. 'That which we call a rose by any other name would smell as sweet.'" When it began to drizzle, he actually said, "The rain it raineth every day." When I turned on the car radio, he commented, "If music be the food of love, play on." There was no conversation. Every time he opened his mouth, he'd be a character from a play. Never himself. At the end of the date, he told me that "parting was such sweet sorrow." Certainly, the sweetest sorrow *I've* ever had.

ROSE, 19, EVANSTON, ILL.

★★★★★★★★★★★★★★ 163

Robert announced that he was going to have a political career and was looking for an appropriate wife. He questioned me about possible scandals in my past, and wanted to role-play a variety of situations in which the first lady might find herself. He'd be a smarmy reporter, interviewing me. Or he'd be foreign royalty, greeting me. Apparently he didn't think "Get stuffed" was a first lady kind of line.

MIRANDA, 22, PROVIDENCE, R.I.

★ ★ ★ ★ ★ ★ ★ ★ ★ ★ ★ ★ ★

We took a day trip to attend an opening at an art gallery. I fell asleep on the train, on his shoulder. When I woke up, to my horror, I saw that I'd left a puddle of drool on his shoulder, on his black silk shirt. I didn't tell him about it and hoped he wouldn't notice.

SUSANNA, 24, WASHINGTON, D.C.

We drove to Montreal, just to explore the city. We took a carriage ride and ate in the old part of the city. It was nice. Romantic. But when it was time to go, he had no idea where he'd parked. I hadn't paid attention; he was driving. We walked all over, looking for his car. Our feet ached. Finally, we went to a rooftop bar in the vicinity of where we'd parked, hoping to be able to spot it from above. But by the time we got up there, it was too dark to see anything. We sat up all night, drinking, waiting for dawn, when we wandered the streets until we found the car. By then we weren't speaking. It was a long drive home.

MARIANNE, 28, BUFFALO, N.Y.

★ ★ ★ ★ ★ ★ ★ ★ ★ ★ ★ ★ ★

We're at my best buddy's wedding and she loses her heirloom emerald ring. Of course they have to stop the dancing and turn up the house lights to have everyone search. Guys in tuxes and women in gowns are on the floor on their hands and knees searching. That night she finds it in her purse. Apparently, she put it there when she washed her hands.

MIKE, 27, DOVER, DEL.

According to Jeannie, if it didn't cost a couple of hundred dollars, it wasn't fun.

KEN, 24, SEATTLE, WASH.

★ ★ ★ ★ ★ ★ ★ ★ ★ ★ ★ ★ ★ ★ ★ *167*

She wasn't impressed that I was a track star in college. So I stopped at a field and decided to show her a high jump. The rest of the evening was spent in the emergency room, setting my ankle. She wasn't impressed with that, either.

MARV, 33, FARGO, N.DAK.

He took me to the races. He won a big bet and was so ecstatic, he started handing out five-dollar bills to strangers. But then he lost three in a row, got depressed, and took me home before dinner.

FELICIA, 33, CHERRY HILL, N.J.

★ ★ ★ ★ ★ ★ ★ ★ ★ ★ ★ ★ ★ ★

We parked a few blocks from the restaurant for my friend's wedding reception. I'd spent half the day getting my hair done and was wearing a satin gown. Halfway there, there's a cloudburst. I mean a sudden dumping of buckets of water right on our heads. Derek started laughing and we ran for cover but, when we walked into the party, Derek looked like a drowned rat. And he looked a lot better than I did.

JILL, 23, OCALA, FLA.

★ ★ ★ ★ ★ ★ ★ ★ ★ ★ ★ ★ ★ ★

He stood up, banged his spoon against a glass, and announced to the whole restaurant that it was my birthday. He called upon a whole roomful of strangers to sing "Happy Birthday" to me. I wanted to die, but not until I'd killed him. Oh, and it was *not* my birthday.

MEGAN, 29, SYRACUSE, N.Y.

★ ★ ★ ★ ★ ★ ★ ★ ★ ★ ★ ★ ★

Spring weekend. Formal dance. I go the bathroom and forget that my gown has a long sash in back. When I get off the toilet, it's drenched. I don't know what to do. I can't walk around with a peed-on sash, but I can't take it off because it's sewn into the gown. So I twist and turn and wash it in the sink, but by then the whole gown's soaking. I turn on the hand dryer and try to blow it dry. This takes like an hour and a half—maybe two—and it's exhausting. When I finally get back to the party, I can't find my date. He's been looking all over for me, figures I've ditched him. When I finally find him, I'm too embarrassed to tell him what happened. Besides, he's too mad to listen. The whole weekend, not just the sash, was a wash.

CLAIRE, 26, ITHACA, N.Y.

★ ★ ★ ★ ★ ★ ★ ★ ★ ★ ★ ★ ★ ★ **171**

Mostly, he liked to hang out naked in the mountains—some kind of primitive, back-to-nature thing. Walking bare-assed through the trees, among thorns and poison ivy—this was, to him, a perfect date.

MARCIA, 22, ELMIRA, N.Y.

I went to use the bathroom in Wes's apartment. He didn't tell me he had a boa constrictor in his bathtub. He waited to hear me scream. He thought this was a hoot.

RITA, 42, NEW YORK, N.Y.

★ ★ ★ ★ ★ ★ ★ ★ ★ ★ ★ ★ ★ ★

I asked Bill if he wanted to go skiing. He said, "Great." He didn't mention that he'd never skied anything but bunny slopes before, so he expected me to stay with him there, and when I wanted to go on to more advanced trails, he stayed in the ski lodge sulking and drinking the rest of the weekend.

SHARON, 27, BOSTON, MASS.

★★★★★★★★★★★★★

Fun to Denise had to involve food, preferably chocolate.

BRAD, 25, MILWAUKEE, WIS.

Fun, for Cindy, has to be about winning. She's the most competitive person I ever met. Everything's in terms of winning and losing. Not just bowling or poker. It's a contest to see who can eat or drink more, get hornier, perform better in bed. I have no problem letting her win.

TONY, 27, PHILADELPHIA, PA.

★ ★ ★ ★ ★ ★ ★ ★ ★ ★ ★ ★ ★

Chuck thinks fun is synonymous with sixpack. And the more fun, the better.

DAHLIA, 21, TOMS RIVER, N.J.

Fun for John had to have shock value. That could mean anything from belching loudly during the romantic part of a movie to showing up at a formal affair with no shirt, only a tux. Or sliding his finger under the table and up my skirt while we're at lunch with his mother.

CATHERINE, 24, BOSTON, MASS.

★ ★ ★ ★ ★ ★ ★ ★ ★ ★ ★ ★ ★ ★ **175**

Hank asked me to a football game. On the way home, he casually mentioned that he had to drop something off at his grandfather's house and said we'd only stay a minute. When we got there, his entire family was waiting for him—four generations, wearing fancy dresses and suits—to celebrate his grandmother's ninetieth birthday. There were places for us at the table. He'd neglected to mention any of this to me. But it seemed he'd told them all about me. They toasted us, and wished us the best of luck, welcoming me as if they were under the impression that we were just about engaged.

KATHY, 33, NEW ORLEANS, LA.

Matthew loves to play his violin for me. It is the single sorriest sound I've heard in my entire life. I'd rather listen to an evening of nails scratching a blackboard. Seriously.

MAVIS, 39, LEXINGTON, KY.

I asked Evie on a study date. She brought books, as if she intended to study. And, here's the weird part: We did.

NATE, 20, BERKELEY, CALIF.

★★★★★★★★★★★★★★ 177

The only thing Leslie enjoys is arguing. It doesn't matter what the subject is, as long as we're on opposite sides. If I agree with her, she changes her opinion, just for the sake of argument. She thinks playing devil's advocate is a parlor game.

STU, 32, WAYNE, PA.

★★★★★★★★★★★★★

Larry wouldn't stop playing the kazoo. All evening. When there was a peaceful moment, a break in the conversation, I'd think, "Maybe he's going to kiss me." But no. He'd blow his kazoo. It was literally spine-tingling.

MARILYN, 30, OCALA, FLA.

On our way to a concert, we're stopped, pulled over by the police. Seems we're driving a stolen vehicle. Seems Leroy forgot to tell his roommate he was borrowing his car.

KEERA, 19, MILWAUKEE, WIS.

★ ★ ★ ★ ★ ★ ★ ★ ★ ★ ★ ★ ★ **179**

Tim took me to see his grandparents. I thought it was sweet. But his grandfather dozed off and slept the whole time we were there. And his grandmother had no idea who he was.

LOUISE, 30, AUSTIN, TEX.

Craig was a wrestler. He wanted to practice his holds. Every so often, out of the blue, he'd lock my head under his arm. Or, I was sitting on the floor and all of a sudden he pounced on me, twisted me into a pretzel and said, "Okay, Doreen, say hello to your knees."

DOREEN, 22, AMES, IOWA

★ ★ ★ ★ ★ ★ ★ ★ ★ ★ ★ ★

He insisted on going to his favorite spots. Everywhere we went, he was like a celebrity. He'd stop to talk to everyone. It would take an hour to get to our table, and then people would keep stopping by to say hi. You'd think he was, like, the mayor. Or the leader of the mob.

TRINA, 29, BRONX, N.Y.

★ ★ ★ ★ ★ ★ ★ ★ ★ ★ ★ ★ ★

I'm a beautician. When he got to my place, he asked if I could cut his hair before we stepped out. I told him I didn't bring my work home. He complained that, since he was paying for dinner, I should buy him a trim.

CHANTELLE, 24, SPRINGFIELD, PA.

Frank took me to a World Series game. Our seats were so high up, you needed binoculars to see the players. He apologized for having only one pair, but he gave me a play-by-play description of what he saw.

CONSTANCE, 27, SCARSDALE, N.Y.

We went to a baseball game. A night game. I'm hoping Amanda'll want me to stay over. But we get back to her place and she realizes she doesn't have her purse. She left it somewhere in the stands. So I drive her back to the stadium. We get a guard to take us through the stands to where we were sitting. Of course it's not there. So I start going through trash cans in the parking lot. Wet trash. I was touching things you don't want to think about. Wads of it. At about midnight, I actually find the thing. No money, but the purse. I take her home and she won't let me in. She won't even kiss me good night. In fact, she tells me to go home and take a shower.

RICHARD, 28, PHILADELPHIA, PA.

★ ★ ★ ★ ★ ★ ★ ★ ★ ★ ★ ★ ★

Hope's favorite thing is to crack her gum. It's like an art form to her.

MITCH, 31, BLOOMINGTON, IND.

Wilson yodeled. At a party, right in front of people.

EUNICE, 40, BINGHAMTON, N.Y.

Tamara's favorite thing to do is complaining. It's also what she does best. It's her talent.

LEON, 34, WASHINGTON, D.C.

I take Peg out to the country, drive forty miles to a state park. It's a perfect day, crisp, sunny. I've got wine and cheese and cold chicken and fresh strawberries. I've got a tablecloth, good crystal glasses, and cloth napkins. We get there, I set up everything, and she gets weird. Before we even eat anything, she says she has to go back—now. Turns out she's got her period. It's all over her clothes. She won't just go to a ladies' room somewhere or a drugstore. Nothing will do but going home. So I pack up and drive her home. She sat wrapped in my tablecloth the whole way, which, by the way, she kept.

NEAL, 23, ROCHESTER, N.Y.

★ ★ ★ ★ ★ ★ ★ ★ ★ ★ ★ ★ **185**

She took me to her folk-dancing club. Wanted to polka together.

JORDAN, 26, CHICAGO, ILL.

Kevin sang to himself the whole time. That Beatles' song "Ob La Di, Ob La Da." In the car, in line, in our seats before the show, after the show. Probably during, too, but I couldn't hear it. But it was "Ob La Di, Ob La Da" the whole night. And the whole next day—no, the whole next *week*—I couldn't get that damn song out of my head. In fact, now, just talking about it, it's starting again.

CLAIRE, 20, URBANA, ILL.

★★★★★★★★★★★★★★

Fun, for Frank, had to be dangerous. This could mean running red lights, eating too many hot dogs, skiing the expert slopes, drinking too much beer, making me mad. Anything to test a limit.

ANDREA, 32, CASPER, WYO.

He brought his six-year-old son along. That was all right; he only got to see his kid on weekends. But he also let his son decide where we'd go—the arcade. He let his son pick the restaurant and order our food. Pizza, pizza, pizza. When we went home, he let his son pick out a video for us to watch. Then he went to bathe him and read him a story. I sat in the living room, waiting for an opportunity to ask him to take me home. When he came back downstairs, though, he didn't want to leave his son alone, so he thought I should spend the night.

SOPHIE, 35, BOISE, IDAHO

★ ★ ★ ★ ★ ★ ★ ★ ★ ★ ★ ★ ★

It snowed for three days and everything was closed—businesses, courts, schools, everything. I was snowed in and lonely, so I trekked two miles in knee-deep snow to Bob's apartment to surprise him. It took me all afternoon to get there, and I was freezing and tired. But when I got there, he wasn't. So I trekked back. When I got home, I found a note on my mailbox. He'd trekked two miles to my house, looking for me. We must have passed each other. Of course, by the time I got the note, it was too late, and I was too cold and tired to go back. Next time, I'll call first.

DIERDRE, 30, CAMDEN, MAINE

When Harry asked me out, he said we'd grab a bite with friends. He didn't mention that we were going to make a condolence call. I didn't know the people. I didn't know the deceased, his name, his age, how he died, or anything about him. It was very sad, though. Everyone was broken up, crying softly. Young people, old people, friends, family—everyone adored him. He must've been a great guy. I was sad for days afterward. What a loss.

FAITH, 22, GRAND RAPIDS, MICH.

★ ★ ★ ★ ★ ★ ★ ★ ★ ★ ★ ★ ★

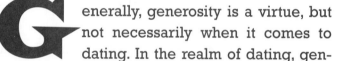

CHAPTER FIVE

★ Giving and ★ Receiving

Generally, generosity is a virtue, but not necessarily when it comes to dating. In the realm of dating, generosity can be a symbolic, political statement of power, attraction, possessiveness, and lust. What and when one gives have meaning far beyond the gift itself; picking up the check—or not—can be interpreted many ways.

In dating, occasions omitted, anniversaries unacknowledged, and birthdays forgotten can be unforgivable. Even remembering can be risky; an opened gift reveals much more than what's in the box. Thoughtfulness, appropriateness, taste, and intention are often inferred from the choice. "Hank bought me Godiva chocolates," Brenda says. "I almost killed him. He's *so* insensitive. He knows that I'll eat them and blow my diet."

Money matters can also be delicate. Sharing the tab can signify mutual respect and equality, or something else. "Money's a language," says Mike. "If she lets you pay, it means she's submitting, letting you dominate. She's attracted to you, saying you wear the pants. If she insists on paying half, she's either not attracted or doesn't want you to know that she is."

Whatever interpretations dates may draw, managing money and giving gifts reflect the dynamic of a duo. Whether your date pays part, none, or all; puts in the tip or picks up the tab; splurges or skimps or skips gifts altogether, the behavior speaks volumes. In the context of dating, the rituals of giving, paying, and managing the material aspects of life contain a language of their own—a language, basically, in which what you pay is what you say.

His shoes must have cost at least two months' rent, and he drove a Ferrari. When the bill for our dinner came, I wanted to be polite, so I offered to share. I was sure he'd say, "No way. It's on me." But he said, "Fine," and put away his corporate credit card. I was trapped. What could I say, that I didn't really *mean* I wanted to share, that it was just *form*, a matter of social correctness? The bill was $226. *Plus* the tip.

LAURIE, 26, NEW YORK, N.Y.

He brought his buddy on the date with him, and in the ticket line, he explained that he was paying for his friend's ticket and popcorn because his friend was saving for a summer trip to Europe, but that I'd have to pay for my own. I didn't mind paying my own way, but I did mind being the third wheel on *their* date.

KATHY, 23, LENEXA, KANS.

★ ★ ★ ★ ★ ★ ★ ★ ★ ★ ★ ★ ★ ★ *195*

We passed a gallery. Paul dropped in and bought a four-thousand-dollar painting. We passed a men's store. He stopped in and got himself a five-hundred-dollar sweater. It never occurred to him to buy me as much as a stick of gum.

WENDY, 35, TALLAHASSEE, FLA.

I met Ned through the personal ads. He said he favored "equality between the sexes." Actually, he just wanted women to pay their own way.

EVELYN, 54, SAN FRANCISCO, CALIF.

★ ★ ★ ★ ★ ★ ★ ★ ★ ★ ★ ★ ★

How cheap was he? He didn't want to pay for a parking lot, so he parked on the street. And, guess what, he got a parking ticket. Stan cursed and said no way was he going to pay it. Then he put it on the windshield of the car parked behind his. I reminded him that the ticket had his license plate number on it. He said, "Yeah, but you never know—nobody reads parking tickets. The guy might just pay it."

NANCY, 23, BOSTON, MASS.

★ ★ ★ ★ ★ ★ ★ ★ ★ ★ ★ ★ ★

When the check came, he asked me for $22.50. I said, "What?"

He said, "That's half. Want to check my addition?"

I had only a ten on me; I'd had no idea he'd want me to pay. When I told him, he offered to walk me to an ATM machine.

SALLY, 31, SYRACUSE, N.Y.

★ ★ ★ ★ ★ ★ ★ ★ ★ ★ ★ ★ ★ ★

He let me pay for the second round of drinks. He wanted to rent tapes and let me pay for both of them. He bought us a medium soda and a popcorn to *share*. He invited himself to my studio apartment to watch them; his place was too "messy." And then, he fell asleep watching the movie and I couldn't wake him up. I ended up trying to sleep on the floor while he snored happily all night on my bed.

CLAIRE, 23, BALTIMORE, MD.

★ ★ ★ ★ ★ ★ ★ ★ ★ ★ ★ ★ ★

For Valentine's Day, he gave me crotchless red lace underpants.

MOLLY, 24, DUBLIN, OHIO

As soon as he came in, Dennis had to make a phone call. He used my phone for about twenty minutes. I figured he had to call his office. When I got the bill, I realized he'd been calling all over the country—New Mexico, Nevada, Colorado. If he'd had more time, he'd probably have called Japan.

JOIE, 33, PORTLAND, MAINE

Michael was careful with his money. He never wasted a dime—he figured the tip to a penny and comparison-shopped for groceries. He'd go to three different markets to save a quarter on milk. And when he took me out to dinner, it was always to a place that offered two-fers. He paid for Valentine's Day dinner with coupons.

BETSY, 23, EUGENE, OREG.

★ ★ ★ ★ ★ ★ ★ ★ ★ ★ ★ ★ ★ **201**

I'd been dating Samantha for about six months. I paid for all our dates. I brought her flowers and bought her earrings for our one-month anniversary, a necklace for her birthday. I brought her souvenirs whenever I went out of town. For my thirtieth birthday, she gave me an umbrella. An *umbrella*.

RICHARD, 30, ATLANTA, GA.

Antoinette borrows my sweaters, shirts, sweatpants, and—poof! They're hers. She takes my socks and my jockeys, then keeps them. I have no clothes anymore.

TERRYL, 38, PITTSBURGH, PA.

For her birthday, I gave her a blank check. I thought it would show her that I trusted her but that I was generous. I thought she'd spend about twenty-five dollars. She spent over four hundred—on jewelry. I guess I should be grateful; she could have bought the store.

AL, 37, PROVIDENCE, R.I.

★★★★★★★★★★★★★★ 203

Everett asked me on a cruise and I thought it was quite romantic—until he explained the policy of ships basing their rates on double occupancy. He said that going alone would cost almost as much as taking me, so I might as well come along. He wanted to get his money's worth. I made sure I did.

EMMA, 63, CINCINNATI, OHIO

Herb brought me a home-grown tomato. One.

CYNTHIA, 28, BRYN MAWR, PA.

★ ★ ★ ★ ★ ★ ★ ★ ★ ★ ★ ★ ★

In all the time I went with him, Lou never had cash. He borrowed from me for popcorn, movie tickets, parking, a newspaper, a candy bar, a beer. On my birthday, he took me to a flower shop and told me to pick out a corsage. The florist pinned it on and gave Lou the bill. You guessed it. He offered me coffee, then asked me to pay. And he never paid me back. Leaving parking lots after a movie, he'd say, "You gotta ten? I'll give it to you next time." After a few months, I couldn't *afford* a next time.

RACHEL, 53, NEW YORK, N.Y.

She earns 30 percent more than I do and thinks this embarrasses me, so she figures out the cost of our dates and insists on paying 30 percent more. *That* embarrasses me.

TIM, 32, NORWICH, CONN.

The day after our date, Cheryl called to thank me for the flowers. Except I hadn't sent her any. And, no, I didn't tell her that.

DICK, 23, ST. CLOUD, MINN.

206 ★ ★ ★ ★ ★ ★ ★ ★ ★ ★ ★ ★ ★

Frank argued with the parking-lot attendant that we'd been in the lot for only an hour and fifty-three minutes, not two hours. He accused them of rigging their meter. He demanded to see the manager and spent almost an hour fighting over seventy-five cents.

HILDA, 48, WINSTON-SALEM, N.C.

★★★★★★★★★★★★★

We were gambling, playing blackjack. I was winning, but my pile of chips kept getting smaller. Finally, I realized that Bob had lost all of his chips and was using—and losing—mine. He said I had no right to complain; he'd staked me my first twenty dollars.

ANITA, 49, CHERRY HILL, N.J.

For Christmas, Al gave me a picture of himself, framed. Like he thought that I'd really want that.

PAIGE, 25, LEXINGTON, KY.

The car was towed while we were at dinner. I had to listen to her say that she told me not to park there. I had to take her home in a cab, then take a cab to the impound, and pay to get my car back. Altogether, with the dinner, cab, impound, and towing, the evening cost over three hundred dollars. She offered to pitch in, and I accepted her offer. She handed me ten dollars. Ten dollars. She thought she was doing a good thing, especially since she told me not to park there.

HAL, 29, ELKINS PARK, PA.

★ ★ ★ ★ ★ ★ ★ ★ ★ ★ ★ ★ ★ **209**

I offered to pay half. He included not just the cost of pizza, drinks, and the movie, but half the parking, half the tip, and a portion of the gas. At the end of the evening, he told me how much I owed him, and offered to itemize everything if I had a question.

AMY, 25, DOWNERS GROVE, ILL.

For my birthday, he gave me a bathmat and toilet cover. What would he give me if we got serious? A whole bathroom set, complete with shower curtain and towels?

JADE, 30, KISSIMMEE, FLA.

For my birthday, Bess gave me two tickets to a hockey game. For Christmas, she gave me gift certificates for two drinks at a pub and two dinners at an Italian place. Everything she ever gave me was basically for herself, a ploy not just to get me to take her out again but to choose where we'd go.

PAUL, 28, CHICAGO, ILL.

★ ★ ★ ★ ★ ★ ★ ★ ★ ★ ★ ★ ★ **211**

Bill sent me cards with kisses and hugs from a secret admirer. Flowers, gifts. Of course, I thought it was from my old boyfriend and I went back with him, thinking he'd begun to appreciate me. By the time I found out Bill had sent the stuff, I was engaged to Frank.

DEBBIE, 30, WALLINGFORD, PA.

★ ★ ★ ★ ★ ★ ★ ★ ★ ★ ★ ★ ★

She offered to pay for the parking garage. Now, in her purse, she carries enough stuff to survive a nuclear war for six months. Not just money, credit cards, and keys. I'm talking about a Swiss army knife, a first-aid kit, granola bars, gum, Mace, toothpaste, toothbrush, mini-bottles of vodka and Scotch, antibacterial wipes, fresh underwear, decks of cards, a camera, a diary, condoms, makeup. And that's just what I *remember*. I had a lot of time to study it all while she searched for our parking stub.

HOWARD, 35, BROOKLYN, N.Y.

★ ★ ★ ★ ★ ★ ★ ★ ★ ★ ★ ★ ★ 213

For our six-month anniversary, he bought me a squirt gun. A squirt gun? Trust me, it got some use that night.

JESSICA, 24, ST. CHARLES, ILL.

I bought her a candy apple. She took a big bite and when she took the apple out of her mouth, her teeth came with it. Her bridge came loose, stuck to the taffy.

WARREN, 34, TOLEDO, OHIO

For Christmas, she gave me this horrible sweater with bears and pine trees on it. I returned it. Now she wants to know why I never wear it.

TED, 29, SEATTLE, WASH.

Hannah bought me really vile aftershave. She insists that I wear it, says it turns her on. That being the case, I go around smelling vile. It's worth it.

MILES, 27, BRAINTREE, MASS.

She gave me an awful, itchy patterned sweater. Just awful. So I took it back to Nordstrom's to exchange it. The clerk sneered and assured me that the sweater did not come from any Nordstrom's store. She must have bought it at some discount store and stuck it in a fancy box. Like what, the box makes the sweater less tacky? Like I'd like it if it cost a lot?

ARNIE, 25, NEW YORK, N.Y.

For my birthday, she gave me a goldfish. One.

RANDOLPH, 32, ANN ARBOR, MICH.

★ ★ ★ ★ ★ ★ ★ ★ ★ ★ ★ ★ ★

Joel gave me a gift certificate for twenty-four hours as a sex slave. No expiration date. We broke up about a year ago, but I'm hanging on to it. You never know. I may need to redeem it sometime.

CAMILLE, 21, ITHACA, N.Y.

★★★★★★★★★★★★★★

Ida never gave anything but practical gifts. In the year I dated her, she gave me a teapot, a new pillow, a heating pad, and a grocery cart. I still use every single one of them, and they all remind me of her.

DMITRI, 57, PITTSBURGH, PA.

He told me that he gives all his dates the same cologne. He said it was amazing how it smells a little different on each of us. And he sniffed me to make sure I was wearing it.

GLADYS, 52, SARASOTA, FLA.

For my birthday, she gave me a box of decorator condoms. I didn't know what to say. Thank you? I'll enjoy them? They'll make me think of you? What?

JASON, 27, ST. PAUL, MINN.

The only thing Paul ever gave me was his opinion. He was real generous with that, gave more than you could ever use, want, or bear to listen to.

PHOEBE, 23, ALBANY, N.Y.

★ ★ ★ ★ ★ ★ ★ ★ ★ ★ ★ ★ ★ ★

CHAPTER SIX

★ The Kiss ★

Perhaps there is no such thing as the perfect kiss. Even so, many continue to search for it, sorting through dozens of partners, hoping to find one whose kiss rings their bells, lights their fires, and shakes their ground.

Before couples actually kiss, however, a lot of preparation often takes place. The foreplay involves complicated rituals of flirting, conversing, preening, and posing. There are flights of anticipation and imagination, doses of chemistry and charisma. Couples dance around each other, teasing with talk, pauses, stares, sighs, timing, positions of the body, tilts of the head, and blinkings of the eyes. They endure the pulsing, the waiting, the wondering, until, finally, one or the other makes the First Move.

Of course, sometimes, the Move flops, falls flat on its face, and ends the whole affair. But when it works, the first kiss of a relationship can open doors to new horizons. "A kiss is a promise," Tyler says. "It's a hint of what's to come. It's also how I decide if anything *is* to come."

While some consider kissing merely a polite way to say good night, most agree that a lot can

be learned from a simple smooch. "Kissing," says Matt, "is basic communication between a man and a woman. It says everything that words can't and allows couples to take stock of where they stand. It's a barometer of the relationship."

Whatever else it is, kissing is often a turning point, a beginning of the physical. With the first kiss, first base has been taken, body contact achieved, and ice broken; the couple can move ahead, explore new territory and maybe achieve the perfect kiss. Or, at least, spend a lot of time trying.

★ ★ ★ ★ ★ ★ ★ ★ ★ ★ ★ ★ ★ ★ **223**

Mike was afraid to kiss me good night. He stood at my door, shifting from foot to foot, saying that he had to go home. I tried to make it easy; I tilted my head up, stepped closer to him, parted my lips. Nothing. Finally, when my neck hurt from tilting, I gave up. Just as I backed away, he lunged and dove to kiss me—and missed, knocking me backward into the wall. It was like dating Clouseau.

CELIA, 59, BOCA RATON, FLA.

When you're out with a woman, sooner or later, there's this silence. This pause. This eye contact. That's when it's time to make a move. Gloria stared into my eyes, searching. The silence grew. I leaned forward to kiss her, and she said, "There's a glob of something in your eyelid. Do you have a cold?"

DAVE, 37, WILMETTE, ILL.

★★★★★★★★★★★★★★★ 225

Griffin declared that, with AIDS and all, it was necessary to be completely open. Then he proceeded to tell me his entire sexual history. But after I heard the details of all his exploits, I didn't want to go out with him anymore. Hell, I didn't even want him to sit on my sofa.

JEAN, 36, AMHERST, MASS.

I couldn't get between her and Puffy, her cat. We went into the den to watch a tape. I sat on the sofa next to her, put my arm around her. She snuggled Puffy.

JOHN, 32, HOUSTON, TEX.

★ ★ ★ ★ ★ ★ ★ ★ ★ ★ ★ ★ ★

He licked his lips before each kiss. We're about to kiss and he licks his lips. It was snake-like, reptilian. Also wet. I backed up. Kiss aborted. Impulse lost.

SUZANNE, 32, SAGINAW, MICH.

Allen told me he was a v-v-virgin and that he only s-s-s-stut-t-t-ered wh-when he was t-t-t-turned on by somebody. He d-d-d-didn't th-think he c-c-could go on if he couldn't get s-s-someone to s-s-s-sleep with him. I told him it was a g-g-good t-t-try but, as far as I know, he's still stuttering.

JEN, 30, BINGHAMTON, N.Y.

★★★★★★★★★★★★★★★ 227

He talked about women's hands, how much he appreciated long, manicured nails and graceful, slender fingers. How they enchanted him. How certain women wove sexual spells with their fingertips. How good hands turned him on. I sat on mine till my fingers got numb. When my drink came I was afraid to reach for it.

JUDIE, 34, DOYLESTOWN, PA.

★ ★ ★ ★ ★ ★ ★ ★ ★ ★ ★ ★ ★

The woman purred. I mean the way a lion purrs after it's eaten an elk. Dangerous.

LEROY, 32, DES MOINES, IOWA

Under the stars, I tilted my head, parted my lips, and closed my eyes, anticipating our first kiss. He planted his top teeth right below my nose, his bottom teeth on my chin, and dug them into my skin. At the same time, he jabbed at me with his tongue. I pulled away, and there was an embarrassed silence. Then he said, "I'm sorry I'm not a good kisser. My tongue's not long enough."

AMY, 23, POCATELLO, IDAHO

★ ★ ★ ★ ★ ★ ★ ★ ★ ★ ★ ★ ★ ★ ★

He used breath spray before kissing me. And afterward, as he left my apartment. And in between kisses, whenever he could sneak a spritz, like every five seconds.

TINA, 28, NEWARK, DEL.

Dave loved his looks. Every chance he got, he admired himself in a window or a mirror. When we kissed, he tried to position himself near a mirror so he could watch.

DONNA, 29, SYRACUSE, N.Y.

She punctuated each kiss with a loud, wet smack. Mmmwchwaaa. The way my grandmother kisses me.

MILES, 24, NEW ORLEANS, LA.

Moaning was her thing. Who knows why; certainly it had nothing to do with the level of our activity. The minute we made body contact, she'd moan. She was loud, and like a horn. I mean, I thought volunteer firemen might go running to the station.

MITCH, 31, RICHMOND, VA.

★ ★ ★ ★ ★ ★ ★ ★ ★ ★ ★ ★ ★ ★ 231

When I looked in the mirror the next morning, I had a hickey the size of a golf ball. It took about a month to go away. I was afraid she'd marked me for life.

BOB, 24, DETROIT, MICH.

In the middle of a movie, Cathy leaned over and started licking my face, like I was an ice-cream cone. I turned to look at her, and she started licking my lips. My face was covered with spit.

HANK, 24, LOUISVILLE, KY.

Cassy kissed with food in her mouth. Like, she couldn't take the time to swallow; she had to kiss while still chewing. This didn't work for me, but it wouldn't have been so bad if she'd been eating something good. But secondhand tuna didn't work at all.

JEFF, 31, SONOMA, CALIF.

★★★★★★★★★★★★★★★ 233

She wanted to kiss big in public. And she had to be linked to me, attached like a tick. Her arm was intertwined with mine the whole night. She wrapped herself around me. If I moved, she moved. If she didn't want to move, I couldn't.

BEAU, 23, HOUSTON, TEX.

JoEllen was nice, but she pierced her tongue. I found that difficult to kiss with. And I didn't think I had the right to ask her to remove the metal first.

T.J., 22, YONKERS, N.Y.

Sunny automatically French kissed. I thought it was premature; I don't think you should French without an engraved invitation. But she pried my lips open with her tongue and forged ahead, relentless.

MATT, 32, DES MOINES, IOWA

★★★★★★★★★★★★★★★ 235

Her earlobes were lined with studs. It made them hard to nibble. Who wants to suck barbed wire?

SETH, 24, SEATTLE, WASH.

When I kissed Donny, I smelled food. His mustache kept an aromatic record of what he'd eaten that day. All I could think about was barbecued pork.

DUSTY, 33, TULSA, OKLA.

Steve had a big, bushy mustache. He also had sinus problems or allergies, was blowing his nose the whole night. Then he wanted to kiss. All I could think of was the germs in his mustache.

JULIA, 42, EVANSTON, ILL.

Penny was not timid with her tongue. She cleaned out my esophagus. Stole my half lunch. I mean, she had me nailed.

DEREK, 23, KNOXVILLE, TENN.

She had a bad cold, maybe coming down with the flu. Then she expected me to kiss her. I walked her to her door and she lifted her face and puckered up, waiting. I had no choice but to kiss her. Besides, shaking hands might have been worse—they say hand-to-hand is the way most germs are spread.

JAMAL, 24, PHILADELPHIA, PA.

Letisha keeps her eyes open the whole time. She stares. It's weird.

ERIC, 24, SAN FRANCISCO, CALIF.

It was like she was imitating some movie, some soap opera, doing lavish French kissing and impressive moaning and groaning, fancy moves. I just wanted some simple, basic lip-to-lip. But I got this stage performance.

RON, 32, DES PLAINES, ILL.

★ ★ ★ ★ ★ ★ ★ ★ ★ ★ ★ ★ ★ ★ 239

Penny chews gum while she kisses. I stole it from her and she got furious with me.

PETER, 39, ALLENTOWN, PA.

Charlene made kissing into a chase. Her mouth traveled. I kept trying to catch up with her, but she was always ahead of me. Her mouth was on my cheek, I turned my head; too late—she was on my neck. I scrunched down; she landed on my ear.

BILL, 34, GLADWYNE, PA.

★ ★ ★ ★ ★ ★ ★ ★ ★ ★ ★ ★ ★

She put so much pressure on her lips I needed to ice my mouth when I got home. I mean, she has some strength there—must exercise those suckers.

DWAYNE, 27, TULSA, OKLA.

I didn't realize there are some lipsticks that just don't rub off, and I'll never hear the end of the day I went back to the office after lunch with Reggie.

BUD, 36, DETROIT, MICH.

★ ★ ★ ★ ★ ★ ★ ★ ★ ★ ★ ★ ★ ★ **241**

Tilly saw kissing as just another arena for expressing feminist theories or demanding equal rights. She wanted to lead. She wanted to dominate. She pushed me around like a subordinate at work. Not for me. I want to get primal. I want to be a caveman.

RICH, 34, URBANA, ILL.

★★★★★★★★★★★★

We're out and she's kissing everyone we see. Like it's a group thing. Each familiar face, each "Hi, how are you?" required a kiss. Every "So long." After a while, her kisses seemed easy. She cheapened the whole kissing event. When I took her home, I shook hands.

GARRET, 23, LANSING, MICH.

I think Roland was trying to wash my tonsils with his tongue.

SALLY, 27, CHICAGO, ILL.

★ ★ ★ ★ ★ ★ ★ ★ ★ ★ ★ ★ ★ ★ ★ 243

Marilyn would not kiss me until she showered, put on makeup, and did her hair. Then she didn't want me to mess her up.

TONY, 27, CHICAGO, ILL.

She wore so much makeup that I was afraid to touch her. Like if I kissed her, my lips might sink into it; I might drown like in quicksand. Or I might get stuck to her, like a bug on flypaper.

CHAZ, 25, MADISON, WIS.

★ ★ ★ ★ ★ ★ ★ ★ ★ ★ ★ ★

We were kissing and suddenly he got all upset. Turns out I'd closed my mouth before he did. He said it was like I'd shut him out. Rejected him. I'm serious.

DIANNE, 31, STAMFORD, CONN.

She messed with my hair. I don't mind a woman touching, fondling, or caressing me. That's fine. But don't mess with my hair.

GEORGE, 40, WINSTON-SALEM, N.C.

★ ★ ★ ★ ★ ★ ★ ★ ★ ★ ★ ★ ★ ★ ★ 245

Donald gave me directions. He told me what to do, how to kiss, what to touch, where to put my hands. He was very exact in what he wanted. When we kissed, he stopped me in the middle and said, with exhausted patience, "No, not like that. *This* way." He demonstrated, gave me verbal instructions, and arranged my limbs. He pushed my lips into position and scolded me that I'd done it wrong. "You need to act like you *mean* it."

PATRICIA, 24, ALBUQUERQUE, N.MEX.

246 ★ ★ ★ ★ ★ ★ ★ ★ ★ ★ ★ ★ ★

My old girlfriend told me that it turned her on if I sucked her fingertips. So, during the movie, I picked up Joyce's hand and started on her pointer. She screamed, "Ew! What the hell are you doing?" The whole theater turned and stared.

LEROY, 23, DES MOINES, IOWA

★★★★★★★★★★★★★★ 247

Sybil's mouth tasted like an ashtray. Forget it.

HANK, 25, CLEVELAND, OHIO

I liked Ted and couldn't wait to get close to him. I mean, until we kissed. It was a lip jab. Like a chicken peck. His head moved forward and popped back, and the long-awaited kiss was over before I could respond—hell, before I could blink.

CHRISTIE, 22, ST. PAUL, MINN.

She wouldn't kiss me unless we were outside. The park, the beach—she said she liked the fresh air and the sky. The feeling of nature.

PAUL, 29, OCONOMOWOC, WIS.

Phil told me that in the Middle Ages, the more you revered someone, the lower the part of them you kissed. Then he got down on the ground and kissed my boots.

ELEANOR, 44, SAVANNAH, GA.

★ ★ ★ ★ ★ ★ ★ ★ ★ ★ ★ ★ ★ ★ 249

Rita and I were kissing in the car. I ran my hands up her face, down through her hair. She suddenly pulled away and her hair came off in my hand. Of course, I realized it was a wig. But by then I'd already screamed and pissed her off.

DON, 52, ATLANTIC CITY, N.J.

250 ★ ★ ★ ★ ★ ★ ★ ★ ★ ★ ★ ★ ★ ★ ★

Alan covered both my lips with his mouth and sucked. I ended up with swollen lips, permanently puckered.

SARAH, 22, PROVIDENCE, R.I.

I like pretty feet. I don't want to get involved with anyone whose feet are unattractive, so before we get physical, I always ask them to take their shoes off, and then I take it from there, depending.

TOM, 29, MINNEAPOLIS, MINN.

I was nervous and felt awkward. I turned to scratch my nose and his kiss landed on my eye.

IRIS, 47, NAPLES, FLA.

Fran positioned herself to make kissing awkward if not impossible. I had to maneuver around elbows and shoulders, or somehow shift my weight around to get close to her face. Finally I realized it wasn't going to happen. She had no sense of body alignment, poor kid.

ROLAND, 33, WEXFORD, PA.

Lisa was full of contradictions. She offered to pick up the tab, which meant she didn't necessarily want me to kiss her. But then she let me pay, which meant maybe she did. Then she talked about other men, old boyfriends and such, so I guessed she didn't. You have to pay attention to women's signals, know when to move, when not to.

MARK, 32, ST. LOUIS, MO.

★★★★★★★★★★★★★★ 253

Wade mashed my lips between his teeth. I had to close my mouth or our teeth would have ground together.

LILA, 22, CORPUS CHRISTI, TEX.

I thought he was a babe, and I was falling fast. I mean, I was steamed. But when we said good night, he kissed my forehead. My forehead! Like I was his ten-year-old sister.

JACQUIE, 20, YOUNGSTOWN, OHIO

My girlfriend asked me to give her a foot rub, then she got mad that I gave her a foot rub. Turns out what she *means* when she says she wants a foot rub is that she wants me to kiss her—which, of course, any fool should know.

PAUL, 27, SEATTLE, WASH.

John gave me an Eskimo kiss. Seriously. He said it was flu season and he didn't want to catch a cold.

JOYCE, 19, BOISE, IDAHO

★★★★★★★★★★★★★ 255

Marsha believes that kissing's the only way to break tension between a man and a woman. So every time I'd get angry, she'd start kissing me, which made me madder. Which made her kiss me more until, sometimes, I'd forget what I was mad about—which made me *really* mad.

ED, 27, STAMFORD, CONN.

256 ★ ★ ★ ★ ★ ★ ★ ★ ★ ★ ★ ★

I'd slipped my hand under her sweater and suddenly a flashbulb goes off, right in my face. Her little brother pops out from behind the easy chair with his camera and, as my date is strangling him, offers to sell me the negatives. That kid's gonna go somewhere. He'll be somebody, if he lives long enough.

LEN, 21, FORT MYERS, FLA.

I really liked Heather, but no matter how we positioned ourselves, our noses were in the way. It just wasn't meant to be.

WESLEY, 27, WICHITA, KANS.

★★★★★★★★★★★★★★★ 257

It was a perfect day at the shore—the perfect place. She was the perfect girl. I was waiting for the perfect moment to give her a perfect kiss. The sun was setting. Her hair was blowing in the breeze. The waves caressed the shore. I took her hand. And suddenly, a bunch of her friends appeared out of nowhere. Boom—we were in the middle of a party. The perfect moment was gone. I'd waited too long. My perfect kiss was lost forever. But I learned from it; that experience became a metaphor for life.

BOB, 26, RALEIGH, N.C.

★ ★ ★ ★ ★ ★ ★ ★ ★ ★ ★ ★ ★

Jerry is a foot taller than I am, so in order to kiss him, I had to tilt my head back at a forty-five-degree angle. On one of our first dates, I got a soft tissue injury, something like whiplash, from kissing him good night.

CISSY, 20, NEW HAVEN, CONN.

On all four of our dates, Charles always kissed the air in front of my mouth. He never made contact—he stayed about a tenth of an inch away. I tried to lean forward, but he dodged.

HEATHER, 40, ST. CHARLES, ILL.

★ ★ ★ ★ ★ ★ ★ ★ ★ ★ ★ ★ ★ ★ 259

He wouldn't let me watch the movie. Every two seconds, he was trying to make out with me. I shoved some popcorn in his mouth. He started rubbing his upper arm against me, breathing into my neck. I leaned so far the other way I was almost in the lap of the lady next to me.

AMY, 24, ST. LOUIS, MO.

260 ★ ★ ★ ★ ★ ★ ★ ★ ★ ★ ★ ★ ★

Joe kissed like he was eating an ear of corn. Short little nibbles, moving across my face to my ear. Then down to my neck and across to my throat. And back up and across again.

CATHY, 34, ROCHESTER, N.Y.

Sean refused to believe that I'm a natural blond and dared me to prove it. That was about as romantic as he got.

ANNA, 32, TOLEDO, OHIO

★ ★ ★ ★ ★ ★ ★ ★ ★ ★ ★ ★ ★ ★

I took Stephanie to a party. We mixed and wandered on our own. When I wanted to get going, I walked up behind her, put my arms around her, and whirled her around into a big, passionate kiss. Only it wasn't Stephanie. It was a woman I'd never seen before. From behind, she looked just like Stephanie, I swear. Same hair, same height. Both wearing black. Really, it could have happened to anybody. But this lady wasn't amused. And neither was Stephanie.

JOSH, 27, PROVIDENCE, R.I.

★ ★ ★ ★ ★ ★ ★ ★ ★ ★ ★ ★ ★

I heard the toilet flush. The door immediately opened and he came right out of the john. The water hadn't run. He ate cheese and crackers. Touched my back, tried to hold my hand. Wanted to make out. And all I could think of was that he'd gone to the bathroom and hadn't washed his hands.

CORA, 45, DES MOINES, IOWA

★ ★ ★ ★ ★ ★ ★ ★ ★ ★ ★ ★ ★

Ellen moved close to me and stared up into my face with this focused, intense look. I thought, She's going to make a pass at me. Then she said, "Would you mind if I squeezed that blackhead?"

BILL, 22, OMAHA, NEBR.

We were on his sofa, watching TV. He nibbled my ear and then yelled at the news anchor for saying something stupid. He nearly blew my brains out.

FAYE, 24, FORT LAUDERDALE, FLA.

I met Wanda at a singles bar. She was real forward and seemed to be real taken by me. I bought her a drink and asked her to dinner. She leans over, touches me a lot. Snuggles right up. After a while, I go to the men's room. When I come back, no Wanda. I reach into my pocket for some cash, but no wallet. I'd been had. Scammed. Taken for a ride. But I learned my lesson: Never take a wallet into a singles bar. Now, if I go, I carry my money in my socks.

LEROY, 25, DETROIT, MICH.

★ ★ ★ ★ ★ ★ ★ ★ ★ ★ ★ ★ ★ ★ **265**

When he dropped me off, he claimed to have a nosebleed and asked if he could come into my apartment to stop it. He came out of the bathroom with a wad of toilet paper shoved up his nose. Then he tried to kiss me.

SHANNON, 24, OMAHA, NEBR.

★ ★ ★ ★ ★ ★ ★ ★ ★ ★ ★ ★ ★

I'd wanted to go out with Phoebe for years, literally, but one of us had always been involved when the other was free. Even so, for some reason, I always thought we'd end up together. Finally, after maybe nine years, we were both unattached. I thought this was It. I asked her out. But when I got the chance to kiss her, nothing happened. I mean nothing. She put her lips up and we kissed. Nothing. There was no spark. No chemistry. No electricity. Years of waiting, thinking I'd marry her, and thud. Nothing. Kiss of death.

RON, 30, NORFOLK, CONN.

★ ★ ★ ★ ★ ★ ★ ★ ★ ★ ★ ★ ★ ★

CHAPTER SEVEN

★ Undercover ★ Investigations

Birds do It, bees do It and, sooner or later, dates do It, too. Unless they don't. And, if they don't, It lurks in the background, hovering, casting a shadow on the relationship. In fact, when, why, how, and where couples do or don't do It can color all else.

On the road to romance, sex drives a good part of the distance. It is, after all, one of the basic forces pulling couples together. And, whether it leads to passing attraction or maddening obsession, hopeless frustration or hot, raging passion, sex has got to be dealt with.

For some, sexual relations evolve gradually, as part of deepening intimacy within a meaningful relationship. For others, sex is a hurdle to be crossed before a meaningful relationship can hope to begin. "Gary had so much sex appeal that I was unable to think of anything but sex in his presence," June remembers. "My brain was muddled. I couldn't talk, focus, or think. My only hope was to get it over with and have sex with him. Once the sex was over, I could be normal again. For a while, anyway."

Sex can be many things—an end in itself, a passing pleasure, a release of tension, a union of souls. Whatever its meaning, It draws couples in and out of love, and causes them to come together and break apart, and, in Its name, otherwise intelligent, dignified adults have been known to perform acts of desperation, foolishness, and true dumbness.

It was the first time we went to bed together. I took off my clothes and lay down on the bed. He lay down beside me and whispered, "You're so beautiful." I glowed, basking in his appreciation. Then he continued, "You have the body of a twelve-year-old boy."

HELENE, 31, NEW YORK, N.Y.

★★★★★★★★★★★★★

We were in bed, his place, first time. I reached my hand under the pillow and guess what I found? He still sleeps with his little blue blankie.

PAULA, 26, PORTLAND, OREG.

When I first reached my hand into Ron's pants, I found a sock. The man had wrapped his penis in a sock. What? To keep it warm? To make his pants bulge? To cradle it? To soak up stuff in case it leaked? What?

CAROLYN, 24, SYRACUSE, N.Y.

★★★★★★★★★★★★★ 273

For weeks, I'd been moving in on Darlene, and I mean she had some body. But when I finally got my hand inside her blouse, I got a fistful of cotton. I was a little mad; I felt she'd been dishonest with me. Set up false expectations.

DARYL, 24, CINCINNATI, OHIO

Her bedroom shelves were lined with X-rated magazines and sex toys—handcuffs, dildos, some halter-type things with chains attached. I didn't know what half of the stuff was. Didn't wait to find out.

HECTOR, 23, MIAMI, FLA.

★ ★ ★ ★ ★ ★ ★ ★ ★ ★ ★ ★ ★

She apologized that she was technically a virgin and intended to stay that way until she got married. I was thinking, Oh no, I don't want to mess with her if she's so innocent. Then she took over and did things to my body no woman had ever done. But she's still a virgin. Technically.

CHRIS, 24, CHARLOTTE, N.C.

He moved closer to me and whispered, "I've never been to bed with a black woman before." As far as I know, he still hasn't.

JADE, 28, PHILADELPHIA, PA.

★★★★★★★★★★★★★★ 275

We're going to bed for the first time, and he whispers in my ear, "I don't prefer intercourse." What does that mean? I'm thinking, He likes bondage? Strangulation? What? The first time, you never know what you're getting into, who the guy is. I'm thinking maybe he's a serial killer, that he "prefers" murder. I'm trying to figure out how to get away, or how to grab the phone to dial 911 when he continues. Turns out he likes oral sex.

STACEY, 23, TOLEDO, OHIO

First date, dinner at his place—a studio apartment. There were about a couple dozen condom wrappers in his wastebasket. Not that I counted them. But, having seen that, trust me, I wasn't inclined to add any more trash to the pile.

ANDREA, 26, SAN ANTONIO, TEX.

★★★★★★★★★★★★★★★ 277

Not even six A.M., we're in the act, and his phone rings. It's a business call from some guy who has a meeting later that day. Paul takes the call, talks about faxes and reports, and cites statistics without losing his rhythm or pausing for a beat. I guess business really turns him on.

GINGER, 36, WAYNE, PA.

★ ★ ★ ★ ★ ★ ★ ★ ★ ★ ★ ★

When he left the next morning, I went into my bathroom to take a shower. It looked like Attila the Hun had just ransacked it, a tornado swept through it, a bomb had gone off in it. I'm not talking about the toilet seat being up. I'm talking about water everywhere—or other liquids. On the toilet seat, all over the countertops. Soaking towels and washcloths on the floor, hair in the soap, stubble and spit-out toothpaste in the sink. And the worst part is that he used my razor and my *toothbrush*. They were lying on the counter in a puddle of soggy tissues.

NAOMI, 27, HIGH POINT, N.C.

★★★★★★★★★★★★★★ 279

It was only by E-mail. Samson and I "talked" about four nights a week. I still don't have the foggiest who he is. I suspect that he's married. But he was sexy, punctual, and interested, and it was better than being alone. And it's low risk. You don't spend any money to speak of, and you can't get AIDS from a computer.

DOTTIE, 48, INDIANAPOLIS, IND.

After we made love, Leila told me not to tell anyone. If her father found out I'd slept with her, he'd probably have me killed.

BRIAN, 24, WASHINGTON, D.C.

We made love. Then Ricky said, "Wicky sweepy. Tuck Wicky in, Mommy?" I asked why he was talking like a baby. He pouted and said, "Wicky sweepy. Don't yell at Wicky." He kept it up all night. The next morning, he put on his pinstripe for work. I asked, "How's widdle Wicky today?" He scowled at me like he had no idea what I was referring to. But every time we go to bed together, he talks like an infant afterward. Makes me feel like a pedophile.

LIZ, 34, HOUSTON, TEX.

After we'd made love, James thanked me and said he'd been afraid he might be gay. He hadn't been with a woman in two years, and then it had been awful. Lately, a gay guy had been hitting on him and he needed to find out for sure if he was straight or not. He thanked me profusely for helping him figure it out. But, come to think of it, he didn't tell me *what* he'd figured out.

SUNNY, 23, ALBUQUERQUE, N.MEX.

Dottie had tattoos all over her body—well, all over the part that didn't show when she was dressed.

C.J., 23, NASHVILLE, TENN.

282 ★ ★ ★ ★ ★ ★ ★ ★ ★ ★ ★ ★ ★

Lying next to me in bed, she bragged that she'd had just about everything tailored. What did I think of her breasts—didn't they seem natural? And her tummy, and her thighs? She suggested I call the guy, to get the bags removed from under my eyes.

KEITH, 48, SOUTHFIELD, MICH.

★★★★★★★★★★★★★★★ 283

There was nothing about this woman that was original. I mean, her body was a testament to the wonders of modern science. Still, you had to wonder, if you got serious, what the kids would look like.

JAKE, 28, PEORIA, ILL.

★ ★ ★ ★ ★ ★ ★ ★ ★ ★ ★ ★ ★

She explained that she only went to bed with younger men and that she was only interested in a sexual relationship. She'd only go with men between the ages of nineteen and thirty, at the peak of their sexuality. She wanted beef. For companionship and conversation, she'd rather hang out with her women friends.

MARTY, 23, LOS ANGELES, CALIF.

Ed slept in a nightgown. It wasn't lacy or anything like that. It was flannel. And only to midcalf. But still.

ELLEN, 31, NEW YORK, N.Y.

★ ★ ★ ★ ★ ★ ★ ★ ★ ★ ★ ★ ★ ★ 285

Julie's mother called while we were in bed. She not only answered the phone, she talked to her mother while we were in the act. And she managed both activities quite well. It was a little disappointing, though, to hear her tell her mom that nothing was new and she wasn't doing anything special.

WALTER, 28, NORWICH, CONN.

Doug worried about his body. Was his stomach flat enough? Was his back too hairy? What about his abs? How did he compare to other men I'd been with?

GRETA, 35, DETROIT, MICH.

★ ★ ★ ★ ★ ★ ★ ★ ★ ★ ★ ★ ★ ★

Rita wasn't just passive. I had to wonder if she was dead, or just waiting for it to be over. I didn't worry that I was keeping her awake—I wasn't.

MOE, 34, BOCA RATON, FLA.

John never took his socks off. Ever. Well, maybe when he was alone. He must have in the shower. But, in my presence, he refused to bare his feet, even when everything else was swinging in the breeze. He said they got cold. But I wonder: Does he have six toes? Webbed feet? Foot fungus? What?

DOREEN, 29, AUSTIN, TEX.

★ ★ ★ ★ ★ ★ ★ ★ ★ ★ ★ ★ ★ ★ 287

Mitch told me he had a low sperm count, so I didn't need to worry about getting pregnant. He was very proud of the fact that, without using birth control, none of his forty or so former girl-friends had ever gotten pregnant. That was about it for our sexual relationship.

JENNIFER, 28, BROOKLYN, N.Y.

Let's just say there were things he wouldn't do. In fact, if the man could have found a pair of rub-ber gloves, he would have worn them to bed.

TAIESHA, 28, MILWAUKEE, WIS.

288 ★★★★★★★★★★★★★

He breathed in my ear that he'd like to kiss anything that bends, that he liked the feeling of flesh closing around his mouth. He asked if he could nibble the inside of my elbows, kiss my wrists. When I told him to get away from my armpits, he smiled and asked if maybe he could travel down behind my knee?

GWEN, 29, WICHITA, KANS.

★★★★★★★★★★★★★★★ 289

As we were in the act, Roy asked if I'd ever had sex using food. He said he'd been to the farmer's market and had great veggies. He seemed disappointed when I turned him down.

LOIS, 42, PHOENIX, ARIZ.

After we made love, he told me that he was relieved because he hadn't had sex with a woman before. What did that mean? That his other partners had been males? Animals? Inflatables? What?

HELENE, 27, OKLAHOMA CITY, OKLA.

When he asked me out the third time, Doug said, "You know what I'm *really* asking, don't you? I mean, this'll be our third date. And you know what *that* means." I suspected that I did, but I didn't want to, and I made sure that I never would.

TOBY, 31, TOMS RIVER, N.J.

★ ★ ★ ★ ★ ★ ★ ★ ★ ★ ★ ★ ★ ★ **291**

We're in the act. The first time. Suddenly, just as I'm about to come, he rolls off me and says, "No. This shouldn't be happening. In fact, it isn't happening. Neither one of us had an orgasm, so it's like it never existed." And he bounces out of bed, gets dressed, leaves me lying there on the verge. I was ready to kill him. When he gets home, he calls and says if I'll give him another chance, this time he won't take advantage of me. I'm wondering what's going on? Hello?

SERENA, 30, TAMPA, FLA.

★ ★ ★ ★ ★ ★ ★ ★ ★ ★ ★ ★ ★

She has animals—a cat, a dog. The cat sleeps on her pillow, the dog on her feet. There's no room, really, for me. I tried to carve out a spot, but it was scary. They're very territorial.

ERIC, 27, PROVIDENCE, R.I.

He called it Edgar, like it was a different person, and he wasn't responsible for it in any way. This was cute at first, but then it got pretty schizy. "Edgar wants to talk to you." He'd wake me up and say, "I didn't do it—it was Edgar."

ANTOINETTE, 30, MADISON, WIS.

★ ★ ★ ★ ★ ★ ★ ★ ★ ★ ★ ★ ★ ★ ★

When I asked him to stay over, Robert told me that he didn't do sex, that he'd personally overcome his sexual drives and achieved a higher plane and hoped we could attain a pure, clean relationship at that level.

**CONNIE, 46,
FORT LAUDERDALE, FLA.**

★ ★ ★ ★ ★ ★ ★ ★ ★ ★ ★ ★ ★ ★

Her dog watched us when we made love. Like a jealous boyfriend. It was more than a little inhibiting.

DEREK, 37, RICHMOND, VA.

Jim was sound asleep, snoring on my sofa—until he missed the last train home. Then he was suddenly wide awake, frisky as a pup. And horny as a ram. I told him to stay on the sofa and I had to lock my bedroom door. He told me I was cruel. When I got up in the morning, he was lying under a sheet, showing me how it resembled a tent, held up by a stake in the middle.

KIMBERLY, 30, PHILADELPHIA, PA.

★★★★★★★★★★★★★★★ 295

It was not an excellent indication when, right before we went to bed for the first time, he said, "It's not the size, right? It's what you do with it. Right?"

LAURIE, 29, PHOENIX, ARIZ.

All of a sudden, Andrew screamed—this piercing, pained shriek, right in my ear. I thought someone had stabbed him, or maybe he was having an attack of some kind. Turned out it was just a climax. But I was afraid to go to bed with him again. I didn't want to shatter an eardrum.

CARYN, 25, ST. LOUIS, MO.

Donna and her girlfriend had some kind of phone signals when they went on dates. So, starting about ten o'clock, the friend started calling to make sure Donna was okay, and she called every fifteen minutes. Donna didn't answer because we were busy in bed. After the fourth or fifth call, the friend panicked and rushed over to Donna's, using a spare key. She and two of their pals came flying into the room. There we are, butt nekkid. They started screaming. Donna started screaming. Scared the living hell out of me.

DAVE, 27, ANNAPOLIS, MD.

★ ★ ★ ★ ★ ★ ★ ★ ★ ★ ★ ★ ★ ★ **297**

Eugene explained that he believed that romantic love could only be achieved through celibacy. He asked if I'd meditate with him to achieve spiritual unity.

JOELLYN, 32, BRENTWOOD, CALIF.

Kyle kept pawing me anyplace we were in public. Like he was telling the world, "Look what *I've* got." He wanted to make love in parking lots, movies, the public library. When we were alone, he didn't touch me.

SALLY, 24, PHILADELPHIA, PA.

Bob told me that doing it in his car made him feel like he was back in high school. It gave him that excitement of doing something naughty and dangerous. So there we were: oldies on the radio, the steering wheel in my ribs. Just like in high school. And the cops came. They busted us, just like in high school.

WENDY, 25, AMES, IOWA

★★★★★★★★★★★★★★★ 299

What I learned from Dwayne's boat is that it's possible to make love while you're seasick.

BRANDY, 24, GRAND RAPIDS, MICH.

He always sleeps at my place. He keeps a toothbrush and fresh underwear there. But he won't wash a dish, change a lightbulb, or take out the trash. He eats, makes love, sleeps. Showers. Uses all my stuff. And when he leaves, he takes my newspaper with him.

LESLIE, 26, TULSA, OKLA.

300 ★ ★ ★ ★ ★ ★ ★ ★ ★ ★ ★ ★ ★ ★

Right in the act, Sheila bit my lips. Hard. I mean, chewed on them. The woman drew blood.

AUSTIN, 44, KNOXVILLE, TENN.

Stacey wouldn't stay over unless I changed the sheets. She made a fuss about it, so I pulled last week's sheets out of the laundry and put them on the bed. She said I had to change the sheets. She didn't say the sheets had to be *clean*.

NEIL, 21, ITHACA, N.Y.

★★★★★★★★★★★★★★

Jim was a magician. Every place we went, he performed. At the hockey game, he entertained the bleachers before the game. At dinner, the whole restaurant. Theater. We never had a conversation. It was always a show. Unfortunately, bed was a show, too. Now you see it, now you don't.

BARBARA, 41, INDIANAPOLIS, IND.

★★★★★★★★★★★★★

When she fell asleep, Eileen wrapped her body around mine in a stranglehold, like a python. I was afraid to move because I didn't want to wake her up. But I finally had to remove her, peel her limbs off of me one by one so I could move. No sooner had I freed myself, rolled over, and settled down than she slid across the bed and engulfed me again. At one point, she was lying on my face. I had to force her off me just to *breathe*. Of course, she remembered none of this. She said she had a great night's sleep.

MORT, 30, AMES, IOWA

★ ★ ★ ★ ★ ★ ★ ★ ★ ★ ★ ★ ★ ★

Before he would come to bed, Trent had to brush his teeth. Then he used his Water Pik. Then he gargled. I lay there, listening to him complete his program of oral hygiene. This was *not* a turn-on.

TAYLOR, 31, SYRACUSE, N.Y.

We're all undressed, beside the fireplace. I think we're going to make love. He pulls out his backgammon set and says, "Ever played nude backgammon? Nothing like it."

PAM, 25, SWARTHMORE, PA.

★★★★★★★★★★★★★★★

Seth had no sex appeal. He was a sweet guy, so I kept on *trying* to be attracted to him. But the more I tried, the less I was. He bent over backward to please me, said he'd do anything I wanted. Which is part of the reason he had no sex appeal.

KATE, 36, TAMPA, FLA.

She E-mails me sexy messages to my office. My secretary howls, passes them around.

CONRAD, 33, NEW YORK, N.Y.

★★★★★★★★★★★★★★ 305

I'm taking a douche in his sink. All of a sudden, the sink comes out of the wall and crashes to the floor, with me in it. He and his roommate hear the crash and come charging in, saying, "What's wrong? What happened?" I'm lying on the floor with my pants around my ankles, my behind in what's left of the sink on the floor. Not to mention the water or the pipes.

LATISHA, 23, ELMIRA, N.Y.

She passed gas and ran into the closet, hid behind the clothes, and refused to come out.

HARRY, 28, SAN JOSE, CALIF.

★ ★ ★ ★ ★ ★ ★ ★ ★ ★ ★ ★ ★ ★

We're reading together in his room. His roommate and his girlfriend start making loud panting noises in the next room. Then they start groaning, moaning. She's screaming his name. Then she's just screaming. He said to ignore it; they weren't really having sex. They were just trying to encourage us to have it, to get us in the mood.

LAURA, 20, BLOOMINGDALE, IND.

★ ★ ★ ★ ★ ★ ★ ★ ★ ★ ★ ★ ★ ★ ★ 307

We went out to the country and parked along a river. The car got steamy, so she opened her window, and—instantly—94,000 mosquitoes flew in. By the time she could roll it back up, the car was infested, and we both had bites from head to toe. I took off, driving like crazy, stark naked, opening the windows and hoping the air would push them out. She was screaming. I was swatting. I had bites on my butt, my eyelids, my mouth, places I don't want to talk about.

RANDY, 21, SCARSDALE, N.Y.

We'd made love and I was about to roll over and go to sleep when Ben got out of bed, knelt, and said his good-night prayers. I guess it was charming. But it sort of surprised me. I felt kind of out of place; I didn't know if I was supposed to join him, or what. I pretended to be asleep.

CHARLENE, 31, TULSA, OKLA.

The next morning, as I'm waking up, Mel asked me if I'd mind if he cross-dressed.

MARY BETH, 28, WASHINGTON, D.C.

Lying in bed, Lois asked me if I was rich. I told her I wasn't. She sighed and was quiet for a while. Then she said, "I guess it's all right. Rich guys are mostly jerks, anyhow." I was falling asleep when she spoke again. "Do you think you might *get* rich? I mean, *some*day?"

KEITH, 28, HOUSTON, TEX.

★ ★ ★ ★ ★ ★ ★ ★ ★ ★ ★ ★ ★ ★

Bob and I waited a long time before we actually went to bed. Tension built up and I was nervous. Clumsy. My hands were clammy; I fumbled and got the zipper stuck on the fabric, and I got a hook caught. I bumped teeth with him, moved the wrong direction, had no rhythm, no coordination, no grace at all. He finally managed to get the deed done, but I was afraid it was so bad that he'd lost interest. I looked at him and he burst out laughing. Rolling. Tears came out of his eyes. He laughed, "Well, Rachel, at least the first time is out of the way."

RACHEL, 31, BETHESDA, MD.

★ ★ ★ ★ ★ ★ ★ ★ ★ ★ ★ ★ ★ ★

Anna is tiny. Petite. A pixie. But when she sleeps, she snores like a freight train. No, more like a charging rhino. It's sudden; the whole bed shakes. Hell, the whole *house* shakes. And then, it subsides gradually, so you drift off to sleep again, and then—bam!—here comes the rhino again. She has no idea. I asked her if she knew she snored. She got offended—I mean, seriously mad.

BRAD, 29, PITTSBURGH, PA.

Stan said he wanted to brush my hair. I thought, How sweet. But he meant *all* my hair.

ADRIAN, 22, BOSTON, MASS.

★ ★ ★ ★ ★ ★ ★ ★ ★ ★ ★ ★ ★

Martha sleeps with a pile of pillows between our heads. She makes love with her head turned away and tells me never ever to breathe on her face.

JONATHAN, 27, RICHMOND, VA.

Trevor loved his dog; maybe I should feel complimented that he talked to us both the same way: Sit. Lie down. Roll over. Come.

LIZ, 38, DOVER, DEL.

★ ★ ★ ★ ★ ★ ★ ★ ★ ★ ★ ★ ★ ★

Quentin talks in his sleep. I don't mean grunting and mumbling. I mean he talks. He says bizarre things—sits up and announces a baseball game, play by play. Tells unseen drivers to get off the road. Answers me if I talk to him and *almost* makes sense. I'll ask him if he closed his car windows, if he wants me to set the alarm, or if he's still awake. He answers, "Yes, sure." I've asked if he actually has no idea what I'm saying because he's sound asleep, and he's said, "Yes, sure." When I'm staying over there and can't sleep, I talk to him. It's quite entertaining, and beats counting sheep.

MYRA, 32, LEVITTOWN, PA.

★ ★ ★ ★ ★ ★ ★ ★ ★ ★ ★ ★

Ed does not sleep. When I spend the night, it's awful. He tucks me in and sits at the computer for an hour or two, messes around in the kitchen, does his laundry, vacuums, watches TV. He says he needs only three or four hours of sleep a night, that he does his best work when others are sleeping. I, on the other hand, need three days to recuperate for every night I spend with him.

CLARA, 40, DALLAS, TEX.

As he was about to come, William yelled in my ear, "Tally ho!" In falsetto.

ALEXIS, 33, BOSTON, MASS.

★★★★★★★★★★★★★★

It was our first time together. I was nervous; there was no chance I was going to have an orgasm. But Jeff wouldn't let himself until I did. It was a matter of pride. I told him it was okay, that I'd be more relaxed next time—just go for it. But no. He's relentless. He works. He tries this. He does that. I'm dying, embarrassed, and the more he tries, the less chance there is of it happening. Meantime, the man is sweating. Sweat is literally raining onto me, into my eyes, my mouth—I'm drowning in it. I figure it's a matter of survival, so I scream, I shake, I tremble, I moan. He grins. He's real proud of himself. When it's over, he sighs, "I told you I could do it. Never doubt me again."

PAULA, 29, SHREVEPORT, LA.

316 ★ ★ ★ ★ ★ ★ ★ ★ ★ ★ ★ ★ ★ ★

She wanted to videotape us in bed. She got out her camera and tripod, and set everything up. This was fine with me until she laughed, "Someday, when you're famous. I'll be able to blackmail you." She swore she was joking, but that was the end of that.

PAUL, 27, NEW YORK, N.Y.

★★★★★★★★★★★★★★ 317

He read an article about women faking orgasms and bragged to our friends that no one's ever faked with him. He has no clue. I'm good. I'm real good.

RANDIE, 28, SANTA FE, N.MEX.

I told Margaret I was gay. She said that was okay with her, as long as I took her out on Saturdays and pretended to her mother that we were going to get engaged.

ED, 36, RYE, N.Y.

Peter rolled off me crying out in pain. Doubled over. He asked if there were sharp edges on my diaphragm; he said it felt like teeth were biting him. I wondered if he had a disease or a urinary problem and made him see a doctor. When the doctor said nothing was physically wrong, Peter examined my diaphragm to make sure it had no cutting edges. His doctor told him to see a shrink. I still don't get it. Peter had been married, has a child, yet he seems convinced that women can have teeth in there.

YASMINE, 29, LEXINGTON, KY.

★ ★ ★ ★ ★ ★ ★ ★ ★ ★ ★ ★ ★ ★ 319

Gordon admired my body parts and compared them to his. He sighed that he wished he had mine. "Look at your legs; they're so smooth. If only mine were like yours." He suggested I leave some makeup and lingerie at his place, so I wouldn't have to carry it with me on our next date. I asked him if he'd use it in the meantime. He just smiled.

JULIE, 31, BALA CYNWYD, PA.

He dyed his pubic hair. He said it looked better blond.

JILL, 32, GAINESVILLE, FLA.

320 ★ ★ ★ ★ ★ ★ ★ ★ ★ ★ ★ ★ ★

In bed, Carol whispered that she used to be Carl. She'd had the operation. She used to be a man. She asked if I could tell.

BILL, 47, BUFFALO, N.Y.

The man had shaved every hair off his body. From his eyebrows down, he was bald as a baby.

JENNIFER, 27, WASHINGTON, D.C.

★ ★ ★ ★ ★ ★ ★ ★ ★ ★ ★ ★ ★ ★ ★ 321

We were lying in bed and Roland asked me if I'd ever done gerbils. I asked him what he meant. You've never seen a woman get into her panty-hose as fast as I did.

EMILY, 25, LOS ANGELES, CALIF.

He asked about other men I'd been to bed with. Was he better? Bigger? Built as good? He wanted a report card. No, he wanted a spread-sheet, comparative data.

CHARITY, 26, ATLANTA, GA.

We went to her place. The bathroom counter was covered with four toothbrushes and a display of designer condoms. Courtesy supplies, she called them. Scary, I call them.

ADAM, 40, DETROIT, MICH.

★ ★ ★ ★ ★ ★ ★ ★ ★ ★ ★ ★ ★ 323

CHAPTER EIGHT

★Traveling★ Music

Bad timing? Bad taste? Bad chemistry? Bad karma? Lots of things can make dates absolutely intolerable. Too dependent, too undependable, too irritating, too dominating. One's got annoying habits; another's habitually annoying. Whatever bugs them about each other, incompatible couples eventually opt to part.

For some, breaking up is an art form, a social ritual to be handled with ultimate finesse. For others, it's as mundane as exchanging an unwanted purchase. "Dating is just like shopping for hats," Jenny explains. "You try on hundreds, but reject most. It takes a while till you find just the right one."

Like hats, some dates flop; others flatter; a few are merely fun. This one looks sexy, that one witchy. And it's so rare to find a perfect fit that, in the course of their dating lives, most people eventually endure experiences of both dumping and being dumped.

The end, when it comes, can be blunt or subtle, abrupt or gradual. It can signal painful rejection or explosive relief, old ruts or new horizons. If nothing else, breakups leave most of us wiser, more experienced, and better prepared to deal with our next relationship—or our next hat, whichever.

She told me she didn't like mustaches. I shaved. She told me she didn't like jewelry. I stopped wearing chains. She told me my hair was too shaggy. I got it cut. She told me I dressed too flashy. I bought new clothes. She told me she didn't like my cat. That was it.

MEL, 47, NEW YORK, N.Y.

★ ★ ★ ★ ★ ★ ★ ★ ★ ★ ★ ★ ★

When I tried to break up with him, Leonard begged me to keep going out with him. "Give it time," he whimpered. "It'll get better." As if our relationship was a virus.

CINDY, 23, RALEIGH, N.C.

I finally told one man, in no uncertain terms, not to call anymore. That night, he came over with a dish of homemade English trifle. "You said not to call," he said. "But you didn't say not to stop by."

GENA, 34, BUFFALO GROVE, ILL.

★★★★★★★★★★★★★ 329

After I told him I didn't want to see him anymore, he kept leaving messages on my answering machine, pleading with me to call him. Telling me how he felt about me, how I made his life complete, balanced him, how he dreamed about me, wanted to take me here or there, do this or that to my body. He read poetry to my voice mail. Sang love songs. Pleaded, begged, cried. Completely humiliated himself. He kept on that way for two years. Finally, he met somebody else, and now I kind of miss him. I got used to having his messages. I counted on them.

FRAN, 24, BOULDER, COLO.

★ ★ ★ ★ ★ ★ ★ ★ ★ ★ ★ ★ ★

Peter broke up by innuendo. He was late for dates, called me by the wrong name. Talked about newly released movies he'd seen that I hadn't. I hadn't seen the movies, but I got the picture.

MEG, 20, ELMIRA, N.Y.

We were in bed, talking. And the conversation turned controversial. I guess I took the wrong side of the sexual harassment issue, because— before I could say Anita Hill—I was out in the hallway, holding my shoes.

TIM, 32, BETHESDA, MD.

★ ★ ★ ★ ★ ★ ★ ★ ★ ★ ★ ★ ★ ★ 331

Carl mentioned that he'd met a girl who looked just like Pamela Anderson. "That's nice," I said. Or something like that. He said no more. I realized that he thought he'd told me something important. Apparently, he thought that meeting someone who looked like Pamela Anderson spoke for itself. What would he want with a regular person anymore?

CAMILLE, 22, CHEVY CHASE, MD.

Bottom line, I couldn't get serious about a man with no elastic in his socks.

LISA, 36, PITTSBURGH, PA.

332 ★ ★ ★ ★ ★ ★ ★ ★ ★ ★ ★ ★ ★ ★

She told me that when she was with me, she was out of control, too attracted. She said it wasn't my fault, but I was bad for her. She couldn't be herself around me, couldn't resist me, had to cling. She said that dating me was like taking a plunge head-first in a swan dive, knowing there's no water in the pool. Now what am I supposed to think about that?

CLIFF, 28, BOULDER, COLO.

★★★★★★★★★★★★★

We had a fight and broke up. He'd left his laundry at my house. The next day, I dumped it on his desk. He called to thank me for doing his wash. Obviously, he didn't care that his underwear had been sitting on his desk for all the world to see. I did get some satisfaction, though, knowing that he assumed I'd washed it—knowing that, for the next five or six days, he'd be wearing dirty underwear.

MAYEBELLE, 33, BATON ROUGE, LA.

He took me to dinner and asked, by candle-light, if I wanted children. I said, "Yes." He asked me if I wanted to get married. Tears in my eyes, I said, "Yes." He said, "Well, you and I want different things. I don't want to hold you back." I thought he was proposing; he thought he was breaking up with me.

CATHY, 26, YORK, PA.

At the ballet, Brendan told me he wanted a ballerina. I wasn't a ballerina. That was pretty much the end of it.

KIMBERLY, 22, WASHINGTON, D.C.

★ ★ ★ ★ ★ ★ ★ ★ ★ ★ ★ ★ ★ **335**

Everett gave a whole speech about how it wasn't me, it was him. I was great. He just wasn't ready to settle down. I was perfect; he was immature. This was our second date. Count 'em: one, two. There was nothing to break up *from*. But apparently, this was his idea of a long-term relationship.

EMMA, 27, NEW YORK, N.Y.

★ ★ ★ ★ ★ ★ ★ ★ ★ ★ ★ ★ ★

Gene assured me that I shouldn't worry about him—there was always a fresh supply of younger women, so he'd never run out of partners. But he said he was concerned that I'd have a problem because, as we aged, eligible men would be in shorter and shorter supply. It was his duty, therefore, to give me a chance to catch one before it was too late.

MARGARET, 45, COLUMBUS, OHIO

Ashton listened to Michael Bolton all day, all night. Enough said?

WESLEY, 29, KANSAS CITY, MO.

★ ★ ★ ★ ★ ★ ★ ★ ★ ★ ★ ★ ★ ★ ★ 337

Sue told me she was breaking up with me because she thought I was going to break up with her. Basically, she said she was ending it before I did, so I wouldn't. I hadn't thought of ending anything, but she wasn't interested; why would she believe a man who wouldn't even admit he was going to break up with her?

BOB, 23, GAINESVILLE, FLA.

Kelly told me she wanted a down-to-earth guy who'd take care of things for her. This image did not suit me. I told her she'd be better off with a contractor.

GARY, 33, CHICAGO, ILL.

★ ★ ★ ★ ★ ★ ★ ★ ★ ★ ★ ★ ★

I had to dump him before he dumped me. If you see it's going nowhere, it's much better for your head to dump rather than get dumped, assuming you like the guy. And, if you do it right, dumping him might get his attention, turn things around. Of course, if you *don't* like a guy, well, you can afford to let him dump you. You can give him all kinds of trouble and, generously, let him be the one to call it off.

JADE, 28, OLYMPIA, WASH.

I put up with the toupee as long as I could. He was always checking mirrors, afraid it would slip, blow, tilt, show. Car windows had to be closed. He wouldn't go near a fan, wouldn't swim, ride in a boat or a convertible, ski, or ride a horse, a carousel, or a Ferris wheel. He wouldn't do anything that might jeopardize his rug. The rug determined his whole life and, eventually, even who he dated. As in: not me.

GWEN, 47, MIAMI, FLA.

We'd been going out for two years. Gary took me to dinner and told me that he had some news: He'd met a great girl. Like, what was I, chopped liver? A few months later, he called from a car phone, asked what I was up to, and said that, well, he had to go, couldn't chat, was in the limo on the way to his wedding. Then, a few days later, he called from his honeymoon. "Char," he said, and he sounded desperate, "I think I've made a terrible mistake." He still calls, asks to see me. I tell him not on a silver platter, that if he comes over, I'll leave. Imagine. He met "a great girl." Indeed.

CHARLOTTE, 31, RALEIGH, N.C.

★ ★ ★ ★ ★ ★ ★ ★ ★ ★ ★ ★ 341

I'm sixty-seven years old and George had me sitting by the phone, waiting for it to ring. How undignified. Marriage is one thing; dating's quite another—you have no authority. I had to call it off.

LUELLA, 67, FORT WORTH, TEX.

★ ★ ★ ★ ★ ★ ★ ★ ★ ★ ★ ★ ★

We'd had an argument at dinner. He told me I was jealous and possessive; I told him he was superficial and immature. Believe me, he couldn't drive fast enough on the way home. The whole way, we didn't say a word. That is, until we hit the deer. The thing shattered the windshield and battered his car before hobbling off into the woods. I told him he was lucky he didn't kill us, and our argument started all over again, even though he had to drive with his head out the window. When we got to my place, I got out as fast as I could. The car was still rolling when I slammed the door.

SOPHIE, 30, KLAMATH FALLS, ORE.

★ ★ ★ ★ ★ ★ ★ ★ ★ ★ ★ ★ ★ ★ **343**

I like to spend time with Bess but our conversations are often lacking. I have trouble with my hearing, and she has trouble with her memory. So she tells me to remind her of things, but I don't hear what it is I'm supposed to remind her. I ask her to repeat herself and she can't remember what it was she just said. We get along, though. We have a good time.

ABE, 85, ELKINS PARK, PA.

After dating Harry, all I can say is never, and I mean *never* let anyone take your picture with your clothes off.

MOLLY, 26, NAPLES, FLA.

344 ★ ★ ★ ★ ★ ★ ★ ★ ★ ★ ★ ★ ★

Jeremy is seventy; I'm sixty-six. We're both widowed. We went out and had a spectacular time, but then he didn't call again. I ran into him in the lobby of our building and he looked exhausted. I was worried about him and told him so. "Look," he says, "I got women in the building bringing me food all the time, ringing my bell, asking me to brunch, dinner, lunch, coffee. I use the stairs—I avoid the elevator so I won't bump into them. You're a great lady, but please understand. I don't think I'll be calling you. I don't have the energy." It's a shame what they're putting him through. I feel sorry for him.

EDITH, 66, ELGIN, ILL.

★ ★ ★ ★ ★ ★ ★ ★ ★ ★ ★ ★ ★

After my husband died, people wanted to fix me up. But I thought, At our age, who's there to go out with—someone who keeps his teeth in a glass? I finally went out with Edwin because I hoped for a nice dinner companion. All evening, he complained about his arthritis, his digestion, his gout. I thought, Who needs another person to take care of? I did all that for my husband, but we had forty years of history. Edwin asked if I'd travel with him. I thought travel would be nice. But do I want to share a bathroom with this guy? I don't think so; that would give me much more information about him than I'd want.

IDA, 73, BETHESDA, MD.

346 ★ ★ ★ ★ ★ ★ ★ ★ ★ ★ ★ ★ ★

Max declared that, if we got married, the percentage of money we each entered with should be our percentage of ownership all the way through. I couldn't see going through life with a calculator in my hands.

ELLIE, 32, PHOENIX, ARIZ.

★ ★ ★ ★ ★ ★ ★ ★ ★ ★ ★ ★ ★ ★ 347

What I learned from dating Janie is don't—I mean do *not*—get your teeth cleaned by a dental hygienist after you've stopped seeing her.

JEFF, 34, ALBUQUERQUE, N.MEX.

Sue was a blind date. It was a disaster. At the end of the evening she said, "Look, I don't feel bad that we didn't hit it off. I think it's good to go out with people I don't get along with from time to time. That way, when I'm home alone some Saturday night, I won't feel bad. I'll think, 'At least I'm not out with *him*.'" Truth is, the very next Saturday, I *did* think that. About *her*.

WALTER, 33, CAMDEN, MAINE

348 ★ ★ ★ ★ ★ ★ ★ ★ ★ ★ ★ ★ ★

What finally got to me about Norm was bee pollen. He used to carry vitamins with him whenever we went out. He had a ritual of lining up all his bottles and taking his pills, even in restaurants. Even on trips. We went to a country bed-and-breakfast for a weekend and he forgot his bee pollen. Nothing would do if he couldn't get more, so we spent the whole morning searching for a health-food store that carried it. The nearest was about forty minutes away. By the time he found some and bought it, the day was over, along with the relationship.

FLORA, 44, PRINCETON, N.J.

★ ★ ★ ★ ★ ★ ★ ★ ★ ★ ★ ★ ★ **349**

His family wanted us to break up because we have different cultural backgrounds and different religions. They tried to bribe him with a trip to Europe or Hawaii. A new motorcycle. Money. Whatever he wanted. After we finally broke up, I saw him driving a Jag. At least I know what I was worth.

THERESA, 27, SAN DIEGO, CALIF.

350 ★ ★ ★ ★ ★ ★ ★ ★ ★ ★ ★ ★ ★ ★

Hector thought that somebody had to be the boss and that the "somebody" had to be him. He forgot that I had veto power.

LUPE, 25, SAN ANTONIO, TEX.

Anytime I opened a kitchen cabinet, Barbara yelled, "What are you taking?" God help me if I opened the refrigerator. This made me think that maybe she wouldn't be such a great life partner.

MARC, 31, HOLLYWOOD, CALIF.

★ ★ ★ ★ ★ ★ ★ ★ ★ ★ ★ ★ ★ ★ 351

I broke up with Harriet and suddenly, she's everywhere. The health club, the bar, the deli— every place I hang out at. She's invaded my whole life. Taken it over. My friends talk to her, not me.

MOE, 41, DARBY, PA.

He stopped smoking for "us." One night he lit up and took a big drag on a cigarette. That was his way of telling me it was over.

AMANDA, 26, BOSTON, MASS.

I thought I was nuts about Angela until we got snowed in at her parents' country house for a weekend. We were stranded, in the dark. Sounds romantic. But it's amazing how quickly you can find out how little you have in common with someone. It's amazing how long forty-two hours and twenty-seven minutes can seem. It probably would have taken me six more months to realize how bored I was with her, but it would have seemed shorter.

RICK, 31, MINNEAPOLIS, MINN.

★ ★ ★ ★ ★ ★ ★ ★ ★ ★ ★ ★ ★ ★ 353

Andrew was mad when I told him I didn't want to go out with him again. He said I'd regret it. For the next two weeks, I kept getting pizzas delivered to my door—at all hours. My sisters and I ate half of them, gave some away, froze the rest. I love pizza. I say, if that's your way of getting even, Andrew, knock yourself out.

FRANCINE, 42, DETROIT, MICH.

I found out James was married. When I confronted him, he said, "Does this mean we can't see each other anymore?"

WHITNEY, 29, SAN DIEGO, CALIF.

When I asked what he did, Nick told me he stole cars. Ha ha, very funny, I thought. Okay, so he doesn't want to talk about work. But we had fun, went out a few more times. Then he suddenly stopped calling. I was hurt, to be dropped without a hint. Then I got a letter from jail.

ARLENE, 33, WEST CHESTER, PA.

★ ★ ★ ★ ★ ★ ★ ★ ★ ★ ★ ★ ★

After our first date, Lou followed me around like a stray puppy. He'd ask me out *weeks* in advance, and he'd ask me out again and again even if I'd turned him down thirty times in a row. It wasn't clear, after thirty-three turn-downs in a row, that the woman wasn't interested. Finally, I insisted that I wouldn't see him anymore—ever. He sent flowers and balloons, and hired an accordion player to serenade my condo.

KEARA, 32, SHREVEPORT, LA.

★ ★ ★ ★ ★ ★ ★ ★ ★ ★ ★ ★ ★ ★

Bob was too good to be true; he flattered me constantly. I thought he was in love with me. We went out every Saturday night for a month— Until he slipped up and raved about the movie we'd seen the week before, except that I'd never seen it. Turns out he was dating six other women, one for every day of the week, doing a number on all of us. He said, "What are you upset about? You got Saturday nights. Prime time. The others'd *kill* for that spot."

SHARON, 39, BOSTON, MASS.

★ ★ ★ ★ ★ ★ ★ ★ ★ ★ ★ ★ ★ **357**

We were at a party with a gypsy reading palms. The gypsy told her she was soon going to meet the man of her dreams, and that she shouldn't get involved because it would lead to complications when he showed up. So she broke up with me, then and there.

DAVE, 32, PALO ALTO, CALIF.

358 ★ ★ ★ ★ ★ ★ ★ ★ ★ ★ ★ ★

Within the first five minutes, she told me she could assess the possibility of having a relationship with her date. And the answer, in my case, was no. So she didn't want me to waste money and time on dinner; why didn't we just have a drink and say good-bye? I thanked her for her candor and suggested that, as long as we were economizing, we should also skip the drink.

MAURY, 34, PHILADELPHIA, PA.

I sent him ten pounds of bologna. I thought that spoke for itself.

MONA, 28, SOUTHFIELD, MICH.

★ ★ ★ ★ ★ ★ ★ ★ ★ ★ ★ ★ ★ ★ 359

See, I'd had such bad experiences with blind dates that, when I saw that Sean wasn't a complete disaster, I was ecstatic. Jubilant. So jubilant that I went out with him for about two months before it sunk in that we had absolutely nothing in common. If not for the initial relief following the dread of the blind date, I'd never have gone to *coffee* with him.

PAM, 27, DENVER, COLO.

She told me she tips her doorman to give her signals when he calls to announce her dates. If he thinks the guy's bad news, he gives her a coded message, like "Angela isn't back yet, is she?" or "Did Angie leave any messages for a gentleman caller?" Then she knows not to bother. But she told me I'd made the cut; the doorman must like me. The doorman was very protective of her. He called, as soon as I got in the apartment, to see how she was doing. They chatted. I cut out, suggested that she go out with the doorman.

WAYNE, 32, NEW YORK, N.Y.

★ ★ ★ ★ ★ ★ ★ ★ ★ ★ ★ ★ ★ 361

When I met him, I was driving my brother's '63 Mustang. It was the car he wanted, not me. It's all he could talk about. When he found out it wasn't mine, it was all over.

BRENDA, 25, CLEVELAND, OHIO

He was so *ugly*, I couldn't resist him. He had such rugged animal *texture*. But when push came to shove, I was afraid to get too serious. What if our kids looked like him?

SYBIL, 27, LOUISVILLE, KY.

I told her I didn't want to get involved, so I thought we should cool it for a while. She took it well, better than I thought she would. She didn't cry or even look depressed. She just wanted to know if, since I wasn't going to take her out anymore, would I mind fixing her up with one of my buddies—Joe especially, but if Joe wasn't interested, Matt would do.

KEITH, 26, DOVER, DEL.

★ ★ ★ ★ ★ ★ ★ ★ ★ ★ ★ ★ ★ ★ **363**

Meg told me she used to drop her pants for every man who said she was cute. But, no more. Not with AIDS out there. She said she asks herself, "Is he worth the risk?" and that the answer is always, always, *no*. So that, basically, was that.

HARRY, 27, CHEVY CHASE, MD.

★ ★ ★ ★ ★ ★ ★ ★ ★ ★ ★ ★ ★

I was determined to be gentle about ending our relationship so I wouldn't hurt her too badly. I rehearsed for days. I was going to tell her it was my fault, not hers. That I had problems with commitment and didn't deserve a woman like her. That she was too good for me. I didn't want her to cry or fall apart. Finally, I called and, before I could open my mouth, she said, "Look, Bill. I don't want to see you anymore. You've got problems with commitment. You don't deserve a woman like me. I'm too good for you." It didn't go as planned—it sounded different when she said it. So I told her a few things that bothered me about her as well. There was some shouting involved. I said more than I'd planned. All that rehearsing for nothing.

BILL, 40, TOMS RIVER, N.J.

★ ★ ★ ★ ★ ★ ★ ★ ★ ★ ★ ★ ★ 365

Sid and I broke up because he wanted me to wear high, over-the-knee patent leather boots and I wouldn't. That was the last straw. He complained if I didn't wear makeup and always felt free to critique my clothes. He asked me to change my outfit almost every time we went out. I'd finally told him I'd had enough. And, as long as we were on the subject, I informed him that his nose hairs hung out and that most doorknobs had less glass than his pinkie ring.

PHYLLIS, 46, MIAMI, FLA.

I forgot about our date. She thought I'd stood her up. The next morning, I find twenty pounds of potatoes and zucchinis dumped in front of my door. I couldn't go out without stepping over a mountain of potatoes. I thought this was a great way to express herself. The best way anybody's ever used to tell me to get lost. I asked her out again, in fact. But she wouldn't go.

PETER, 33, ALBANY, N.Y.

After dating Brad for six months, I told him I wanted to get married. He told me that that was impossible, because he already was.

YVONNE, 31, PITTSBURGH, PA.

★ ★ ★ ★ ★ ★ ★ ★ ★ ★ ★ ★ ★ ★ 367

He liked blondes. I was a brunette. So I dyed my hair. He liked small noses; mine was big. I had it fixed. He liked skinny girls. I had a breast reduction and went on a diet. He didn't like condoms; I took the pill. He had no more excuses. I'd become his dream. He decided he likes short girls. I'm five foot nine.

CLAIRE, 30, ST. CHARLES, ILL.

★ ★ ★ ★ ★ ★ ★ ★ ★ ★ ★ ★ ★

I was nuts about Harvey and made the mistake of telling him. He didn't call me for two years. When he called, he acted like no time had passed, as if we were still going together. He asked if I'd go away with him for the weekend. I didn't mention anything about his behavior, our relationship, or my new boyfriend. I just asked him if I could bring the baby. I could actually hear him gulp. He started stuttering and pretended he had to take another call. I don't actually *have* a baby, but he doesn't know that.

SYDNEY, 31, SPOKANE, WASH.

★ ★ ★ ★ ★ ★ ★ ★ ★ ★ ★ ★ ★ ★ 369

Joe left a message on my voice mail, telling me I should check myself for crabs. That was the last I heard from him. He didn't dare call again.

WENDY, 24, CLEVELAND, OHIO

The only thing he saw in me was that I couldn't care less about him. I never even thought about him; that drove him nuts. When he called, I never recognized his voice; he found that captivating. He said that that there was something irresistible about a woman who didn't give a hoot. I said that was crazy and I wouldn't see him anymore; he asked if I'd move in with him.

ABBEY, 33, NEW ORLEANS, LA.

370 ★★★★★★★★★★★★★★

We were having supper at her place and who drops by but her ex. He's annoyed about something she said to somebody and they start arguing. I finish my drink. I finish hers. I have another. They don't notice me. It's like I'm invisible. I doze on the sofa, watch some TV. They're standing behind me, yelling about who paid for the television. I got myself a beer for the road, and they were still at it when I let myself out.

KENNETH, 30, AMES, IOWA

★ ★ ★ ★ ★ ★ ★ ★ ★ ★ ★ ★ ★ ★ 371

He didn't want a confrontation, so he left me a note on my windshield. It told me not to be upset; there were plenty of fish in the sea. So I went to the fish store, wrapped a red ribbon around a dead trout, and had a kid from work deliver it to his office with a note telling him to enjoy. He loved it and called to thank me. He thought it was serious, a friendly way to end. He didn't get it.

EVELYN, 31, KANSAS CITY, MO.

★★★★★★★★★★★★

Terri sent me a CD of Christian rock songs with a note telling me she hoped I'd see the light and find Jesus. She said otherwise she'd miss me, since I was going to go to hell.

CLAY, 26, SHREVEPORT, LA.

After our second date, James told me that he was actually bisexual and, since I wasn't interested in my ex-husband anymore, would I mind if he called him?

AUTUMN, 38, LEXINGTON, KY.

★ ★ ★ ★ ★ ★ ★ ★ ★ ★ ★ ★ ★ 373

Max approached me at a friend's party, saying, "This may sound crazy, but I feel as if I already know you. It's as if I'm going to marry you."

It did sound crazy, but I spent the evening with him. We stayed out until three, and when he took me home, he proposed. I told him we'd sleep on it. Max stayed on my sofa.

When I woke up the next morning, I found no Max, just a note from my roommate. She said she hoped I'd understand, but she'd run off with him. Seems Max told her that he felt as if he already knew her, as if he was going to marry her.

LORENE, 41, FRAMINGHAM, MASS.

374 ★ ★ ★ ★ ★ ★ ★ ★ ★ ★ ★ ★

When we broke up, we were both ready to split. But he had to act like it was all *his* decision. He said, "Sorry, babe. You just don't knock my socks off."

Well, maybe not his socks, but I'd certainly done a number on the rest of his clothes.

DEBBIE, 27, TACOMA, WASH.

★ ★ ★ ★ ★ ★ ★ ★ ★ ★ ★ ★ ★ ★ **375**

He showed up on my doorstep the morning after our first date. He said, "Don't take this wrong, but going out with you showed me that I really want to be with my ex." Not that anything was wrong with me, mind you, just that our date made him realize how much he missed her. He said, "I don't want you to be waiting for me to call and wondering what happened." He thanked me, kissed me, gave me a box of chocolates. What a charming guy.

BETH, 37, CAMBRIDGE, MASS.

★ ★ ★ ★ ★ ★ ★ ★ ★ ★ ★ ★ ★